The short guide to environmental policy

Carolyn Snell and Gary Haq

D1448548

First published in Great Britain in 2014 by

Policy Press
University of Bristol
6th Floor
Howard House
Queen's Avenue
Clifton
Bristol BS8 1SD
UK
t: +44 (0)117 331 5020
f: +44 (0)117 331 5367
pp-info@bristol.ac.uk
www.policypress.co.uk

North America office:
Policy Press
c/o The University of Chicago Press
1427 East 60th Street
Chicago, IL 60637, USA
t: +1 773 702 7700
f: +1 773-702-9756
sales@press.uchicago.edu
www.press.uchicago.edu

British Library Cataloguing in Publication Data
A catalogue record for this book is available from the British Library.

Library of Congress Cataloging-in-Publication Data
A catalog record for this book has been requested.

ISBN 978 1 44730 717 4 paperback

Cover design by Policy Press
Front cover image kindly supplied by www.alamy.com
Printed and bound in Great Britain by Hobbs, Southampton
Policy Press uses environmentally responsible print partners.

FSC
www.fsc.org
MIX
Paper from
responsible sources
FSC® C020438

For

Macy Maren Snell

and

Arabella Lucia Haq

Contents

Figures, tables and boxes

Figures

Tables

Boxes

Acronyms

AAUs	assigned amount units
BSE	bovine spongiform encephalopathy
CDM	clean development mechanism
CER	certified emission reductions
CFCs	chlorofluorocarbons
COP	Conference of Parties
DEFFRA	Department for Environment and Rural Affairs (UK)
DfT	Department for Transport (UK)
EMAS	Eco-Management and Auditing Scheme
ERUs	emission reduction units
EU	European Union
FAO	Food and Agricultural Organization of the UN
FoE	Friends of the Earth
FSC	Forestry Stewardship Council
GCF	Green Climate Fund
GDP	gross domestic product
GEF	Global Environmental Facility
GEO	Global Environmental Outlook
GHG	greenhouse gas
GM	genetic modification
IMF	International Monetary Fund
IPCC	Intergovernmental Panel on Climate Change
IUCN	International Union for Conservation of Nature
JI	joint implementation
KP	Kyoto Protocol
KSI	killed or seriously injured (UK Transport)
MBIs	market-based instruments
MDGs	Millennium Development Goals
MEA	Millennium Ecosystem Assessment
NEF	New Economics Foundation
NEPIs	new environmental policy instruments
NGO	non-governmental organisation
NIMBY	not in my back yard

OECD	Organisation for Economic Cooperation and Development
POP	persistent organic pollutant
RMUs	removal units
SSK	sociology of scientific knowledge
SSE	steady-state economy
TfL	Transport for London
UN	United Nations
UNCED	United Nations Conference on Environment and Development
UNCHE	United Nations Conference on the Human Environment
UNEP	United Nations Environment Programme
UNFCCC	United Nations Framework Convention on Climate Change
UV	ultraviolet
WCED	World Commission on Environment and Development
WFP	World Food Programme
WHO	World Health Organization
WTO	World Trade Organization
WWF	World Wildlife Fund

Online resources

Chapter 2

IPCC (www.ipcc.ch/)
UNEP (www.unep.org)
WHO (www.who.int)

Chapter 3

New Economics Foundation (www.neweconomics.org/)
Environmental Justice Foundation (http://ejfoundation.org/)
World Health Organisation (www.who.int)

Chapter 4

The EU and environmental policy (http://ec.europa.eu/environment/
  index_en.htm)
United Nations Environment Programme (www.unep.org/)
United Nations Development Programme
  (www.undp.org/content/undp/en/home.html)
Commission on Sustainable Development
  (http://sustainabledevelopment.un.org/csd.html)
Food and Agricultural Organisation (www.fao.org/home/en/)
Intergovernmental Panel on Climate Change (www.ipcc.ch/)

Chapter 5

Sustainable development commission (UK)
  (www.sd-commission.org.uk/)
International Institute for Sustainable
  Development (www.iisd.org/sd/)
Involve: making participation count (UK) (www.involve.org.uk/)

Chapter 6

United Nations Department of Economic and Social Affairs
  (www.un.org/en/development/desa/index.html)
United Nations Population Division
  (www.un.org/en/development/desa/population/)
United Nations Environment Programme (www.unep.org/)
New Economics Foundation (www.neweconomics.org/)

Notes on authors

Carolyn Snell is a lecturer in social policy in the Department of Social Policy and Social Work at the University of York, UK. Carolyn specialises in the links between social policy and the environment and runs two specialist modules, 'Sustainable Development and Social Inclusion' and 'Environmental Policy from Global to Local'. Carolyn's main research interests are fuel poverty, education for sustainable development, public participation in policy development, and environmental attitudes and behaviours.

Gary Haq is a human ecologist and senior research associate at the Stockholm Environment Institute based in the Environment Department at the University of York, UK. Gary has worked on a range of environmental issues in Africa, Asia and Europe. His research has contributed to bridging the gap between science and policy at the global, national, European and local level.

Acknowledgements

We would like to thank Sarah Royston (née Hards), Adriana Ford-Thompson and Jessica Roberts for a number of the case studies included in this guide. We are also grateful to Claire Quinn for input when some of the materials included in this book were part of an online MA module in environmental policy. Thank you also to Pat and Mike Snell for providing a quiet writing venue during the summer of 2012. Finally we would to thank to Ian, John, Ben, and Heidi Folland for support their throughout 2011–13.

Preface

In 2011 the Departments of Social Policy and Social Work, Politics, and Environment at the University of York (UK) introduced an undergraduate module entitled 'Environmental Policy Global to Local'. The module covered a range of policy issues and theoretical concepts at different levels of policy making. Students were from diverse academic backgrounds and it soon became clear that there was no single text that could provide a brief introduction to the key issues related to environmental policy. To address this gap the authors set out to write this short guide to environmental policy. This guide has been developed for any newcomer to the subject and anyone interested in how post-war environmental policy has developed and in future policy challenges. We have also provided suggestions for additional reading for those wishing to explore further ideas and key issues discussed. Wherever possible we have added case study boxes developed from our own research, or written by colleagues.

We have found researching and writing this short guide a useful process, and we hope it will be of use to you.

Carolyn Snell and Gary Haq
York, August 2013

1

The environment as a policy issue

Introduction

Some have argued that the rate and scale of human-induced global environmental change is so significant that it now constitutes a new geological epoch in the Earth's history called the Anthropocene (Zalasiewicz et al, 2011; Steffen et al, 2011). The acceleration of human pressure on the Earth's system has caused critical global, regional and local thresholds to be exceeded. Since these thresholds are strongly connected, crossing one threshold may seriously threaten our ability to stay within safe levels of the others. This could have irreversible effects on the life-support function of the planet with adverse implications for human health and wellbeing (Rockström et al, 2011).

More than ever, there is a need to have appropriate and effective environmental policies to make the transition to a low carbon and sustainable society. Policies that address the challenges of climate change, biodiversity, food, water and energy insecurity and environmental pollution are required. This short guide provides a concise introduction to the development, formulation and implementation of post-war environmental policies. It covers a broad range of issues including:

- contemporary environmental issues and their impact on human health and wellbeing;
- socio-economic perspectives on addressing environmental issues and how these relate to the formulation and implementation of environmental policies;

1

■ approaches that have been taken to address environmental degradation at different policy levels.

This chapter introduces some of the main topics relevant to the study of environmental policy, outlining how the subject has grown in importance since the 1960s. It highlights the most influential publications, conferences, agreements and key terms that will be referred to throughout the rest of the book.

How the environment has become a policy issue

Over the last 60 years modern environmental awareness has increased with the emergence of new environmental issues. In the 1950s the great London smog (1952) demonstrated that levels of urban air pollution could no longer be tolerated and led to public demand for clean air. By the 1960s, there was rising public concern of the environmental impact of nuclear power and pesticide use. This was followed by acid rain and the depletion of the ozone layer in the 1970s and biodiversity loss and climate change in the 1980s, 1990s and 2000s.

Media coverage of dramatic environmental events has been instrumental in raising public concerns over environmental damage. The first image of Earth rising in the vast darkness of space over a lunar landscape was taken by Apollo 8 in December 1968. This became an iconic image that transformed public understanding of humanity's place in the universe. In March 1967, the first major oil spill in Britain occurred when the super tanker Torrey Canyon struck a reef between the UK mainland and the Isles of Scilly. The resulting oil slick covered 120 miles of Cornish coast, killing tens of thousands of birds. Two years later, in 1969, an explosion on the Union Oil Company oil platform, six miles off the coast of Santa Barbara in California, resulted in the release of hundreds of thousands of gallons of crude oil. These were followed by other major environmental events which have included Amoco Cadiz oil disaster (France), discovery of toxic waste in the Love Canal Neighbourhood (USA) (1973), Seveso industrial accident (Italy) (1976), Three Mile Island nuclear disaster (USA) (1979), Union

Carbide Bhopal disaster (India) (1984), Chernobyl nuclear power plant explosion (Ukraine) (1987), Exxon Valdez oil spill (Alaska) (1989) and BP Deepwater Horizon (Gulf of Mexico) (2010). These environmental disasters provided visually dramatic news stories, and served as timely reminders of the human impact on the environment.

Environmental concern has been also shaped by other social and political drivers associated with the post-war era. Indeed, it is argued that modern environmental concern developed in the 1960s with the emergence of a counter-culture that increasingly questioned established values and institutions. This was driven by a new generation of young, openly critical and rebellious people (Haq and Paul, 2012). Links were made to social and environmental concerns such as war, nuclear testing and pesticide use. Over the next decade a number of environmental campaign groups were established such as Environmental Defense Fund, Friends of the Earth (FoE) and Greenpeace which were to become influential in shaping public opinion. In 1970 an estimated 20 million people participated in the first US Earth Day that was held on 22 April. The day was marked by a national 'teach-in' led by schools, colleges and universities and community groups. A year later, in 1971 the UK FoE launched its first campaign with a publicity stunt outside the headquarters of Schweppes. The campaign was against non-returnable bottles linking to a wider message about wastefulness and the throw-away society. These groups undertook high profile campaigns and highlighted global issues such as transboundary air pollution, habitat destruction and endangered wildlife. They used a combination of science, powerful imagery and new campaign tactics to bring about changes in public attitudes, commercial behaviour and government policy.

During the 1970s and 1980s green politics became more explicit as campaigners linked social and environmental agendas to create new political parties across Europe in Germany, Sweden and France. Sweden's Miljöpartiet de gröna was among the first green parities to secure national electoral success in Europe. Founded in 1981, it took less than a decade to establish itself on the national scene (McCormick, 1989). Likewise, between 1987 and 1990 the (West) German Greens

Die Grunen held 44 seats in the national parliament (Müller-Rommel, 1994). The 1980s saw the emergence of a new wave of high-profile grassroots and community-based movements that lacked confidence in established environmental groups. These included US environmental justice and UK anti-road movements. By the 1990s a new global countercultural movement had developed which addressed concerns of global economic and trade agreements. Campaigners from trade justice, development and environment communities came together to protest against the policies of the International Monetary Fund (IMF), World Bank and the World Trade Organisation (WTO). Following the turn of the millennium the issue of climate change provided the impetus for the development of innovative partnerships and coalitions between different campaign groups. In the UK, FoE's 2005 Big Ask campaign brought a number of groups together to help to create public momentum needed for the UK government to adopt the 2008 Climate Change Act, which set the world's first legally binding targets to reduce six greenhouse gases by 80 per cent by 2050 compared to a 1990 baseline (FoE, 2007).

A number of publications have also influenced our environmental understanding and awareness while stimulating debate. These include Kenneth E Boulding's concept of Spaceship Earth, Rachel Carson's study on pesticide use, Garrett Hardin's 'Tragedy of the commons', Paul R. Ehrlich's 'The population bomb revisited' and Donella H. Meadows and colleagues' Limits to growth. US biologist Rachel Carson's Silent spring (1962) was one of the first publications that brought the ecological impact of pesticide use to widespread public attention. It succeeded in translating fundamental ecological principles into clear environmental messages. She wrote about 'man's assault on the environment' and saw pesticides as 'elixirs of death'. It also challenged big business and the idea that science could be used to control nature (Haq and Paul, 2012).

In 1967, Garrett Hardin developed the notion of 'the tragedy of the commons' to explain the problem of environmental pollution (see Box 1.1). A common grazing land was synonymous with those parts of the Earth's surface that are beyond national jurisdictions. These 'global commons' include the atmosphere, open oceans and its living resources, Antarctica and outer space. Hardin's ideas have been used to support the privatisation of commonly owned resources and the rationalisation of central government control of all common pool resources (for example, fisheries, groundwater basins and irrigation systems). However, it should be noted that Hardin's commons analogy has been criticised because it ignores the powerful sense of community obligation that could exist and act as a deterrent for abuse of common resources. According to Ostrom (1990), an approach to resolving the problems of the commons is the design of durable cooperative institutions that are organised and governed by the resource users themselves.

Box 1.1: Tragedy of the commons

Garrett Hardin used the analogy of a common grazing land to illustrate that sharing common resources leads to overuse. Each herdsman as a rational individual seeks to maximise his gain. By adding one more animal to the common land the herdsman will gain benefits while the overgrazing caused by the additional animal will have a detrimental effect on other herdsmen who use the land. The rational herdsman concludes that he would benefit from adding another animal to the common land. If this is the conclusion of all the herdsmen it will ultimately lead to the 'tragedy' as each herdsman is locked into a system that compels him to increase his herd without limit. The polluter as a 'rational man' will come to the same conclusion as the herdsmen, that the cost of polluting can be less than the treatment or abatement of polluting emissions. Hardin concludes that *'freedom on the commons could bring ruin to all because we are locked into a system of "fouling our own nest" so long as we behave as independent rational, free-enterprises'.* His solution was 'mutual coercion mutually agreed upon.'

(Hardin, 1968)

Paul R Ehrlich's The population bomb (1968) directly linked population growth to the Earth's capacity to sustain humankind. This was published at a time when the world was experiencing the highest rate of population growth. In 1972 Meadows et al's *Limits to growth* raised wider anxieties about the future of the planet and its ability to sustain human life. The report examined the interaction of five subsystems of the global economic system: population, food, industrial production, pollution and consumption of non-renewable resources. It concluded that present unabated rise in the global population growth would limit the growth on the planet and result in an uncontrollable decline in population and industrial capacity.

A range of alternative 'green' futures have been put forward. These include the publication of EF Schumacher's *Small is beautiful* (see Chapter Three) and the Ecologist Magazine's *Blueprint for survival*, which outlined a manifesto for societal change endorsed by scientists and academics. In 1980 the former West German Chancellor, Willy Brandt, chaired a commission on international development and published *North–South: A programme for survival*. The report outlined a comprehensive strategy for the restructuring of the global economic order and reinforced the extent of mutual interests on developmental and environmental issues.

Three years later, the United Nations set up the World Commission on Environment and Development (WCED) led by Norwegian Prime Minister Gro Harlem Brundtland. WCED published *Our common future* often referred to as the 'Brundtland report' (WCED, 1987). This groundbreaking report reframed the link between environment and development and introduced the concept of sustainable development. The Brundtland report was followed by numerous reports such as United Nations Environment Programme's (UNEP) Global Environmental Outlook (GEO) reports (1997, 1999, 2002, 2007, and 2012) on the state of the global environment. The 2005 *Millennium ecosystems assessment* examined the consequences of ecosystem change for human wellbeing. The Intergovernmental Panel on Climate Change (IPCC) produced a number of reports on the scientific evidence on human-induced global warming (1990, 1995, 2001, 2007b and 2013) while The Stern review (2006) examined the economic impact of climate change.

The factors discussed above have contributed to our awareness and understanding of the human impact on the environment and influenced how policies have been developed and formulated to address particular environmental issues. However, public and political interest in the environment has ebbed and flowed with wider societal changes such as the state of the global economy. The rise and fall of interest in environmental issues has been described as an 'issue-attention cycle' (Downs, 1972). Typically, environmental problems come to prominence due to scientific discovery. Campaign groups demand rapid action, but the problem is costly and difficult to address. Over time, the public and the media lose interest, and the problem gradually fades from the public consciousness. Any recurrences of publicity tend to be brief, having lost their novelty factor. While environmental regulation and the introduction of standards and limits have improved environmental quality, many environmental issues remain unresolved.

Policy responses

International level action

Since the 1960s international action to global environmental problems has gathered momentum. There have been a number of influential global conferences that have resulted in the development of protocols and conventions which have attempted to address particular environmental issues (see Table 1.1)

The international community first recognised the deterioration of the environment as an issue in its own right at the 1972 United Nations Conference on the Human Environment (UNCHE) held in Stockholm, Sweden. The Conference provided a catalyst for the introduction of multilateral environmental agreements and initiated a new era of global environmental governance. It also brought together poverty, development and the environment for the first time. Following the

Table 1.1: Key conferences, treaties, conventions and protocols

1968 Intergovernmental Conference for Rational Use and Conservation of the Biosphere (UNESCO)
1972 UN Conference on the Human Environment and UNEP.
1975 CITES, the Convention on International Trade in Endangered Species of Flora and Fauna, comes into force.
1976 Habitat, the UN Conference on Human Settlements
1977 UN Conference on Desertification is held.
1979 Convention on Long-Range Transboundary Air Pollution is adopted.
1980 World Conservation Strategy released by the International Union for the Conservation of Nature (IUCN).
1980 Global 2000 report is released.
1982 UN Convention on the Law of the Sea is adopted.
1982 The UN World Charter for Nature adopts the principle that every form of life is unique and should be respected regardless of its value to humankind.
1985 Meeting in Austria of the World Meteorological Society, UNEP and the International Council of Scientific Unions
1987 *Our Common Future* (Brundtland Report)
1987 Montreal Protocol on Substances that Deplete the Ozone Layer is adopted
1988 Intergovernmental Panel on Climate Change (IPCC) is established
1991 Global Environment Facility is established
1992 Earth Summit. UN Conference on Environment and Development (UNCED) is held in Rio de Janeiro.
1993 First meeting of the UN Commission on Sustainable Development
1997 Kyoto protocol negotiated
2000 UN Millennium Development Goals.
2002 World Summit on Sustainable Development is held in Johannesburg
2005 Millennium Ecosystem Assessment is released
2005 Kyoto Protocol enters into force
2007 Montreal Protocol on Substances that Deplete the Ozone Layer
2009 Copenhagen climate negotiations.
2010 The Economics of Ecosystems and Biodiversity final report
2011 Climate change negotiations in Durban.
2012 Rio +20

Source: Adapted from IISD, 2012

Stockholm conference a number of national governments created departments for the environment and introduced environmental legislation. The UNCHE also established the UNEP. The Stockholm Conference was followed by the 1992 United Nations Conference on the Environment Development (UNCED) held in Rio de Janiero, Brazil, also known as the 'Rio Earth Summit' which led the adoption of the United Nations Framework Convention on Climate Change (UNFCCC), the Convention on Biological Diversity and a global plan of action to promote sustainable development called Agenda 21. UNCED was followed by the 2002 World Summit on Sustainable Development in Johannesburg (South Africa) and the United Nations Conference on Sustainable Development in 2012 in Rio de Janeiro.

Many of the developments on the international stage have influenced (or indeed mirrored) policy and institutions at the national and supranational level. The development of EU environmental policy and legislative frameworks has produced a unique 'actor' in terms of international negotiations (Carter, 2007). Table 1.2 highlights some of the key events at the EU level, many of which have been influenced by international activities (for example much of EU level action on climate change has been influenced by agreements under the United Nations Convention on Climate Change).

Thinking about policy responses: sustainable development

With our increased understanding of the causes of specific environmental problems there has also been a shift in thinking among policy makers in terms of how development should occur. The Brundtland Commission report, *Our common future*, attempted to link economy–society–environment and defined the term 'sustainable development' as: 'development that meets the needs of the present without compromising the ability of future generations to meet their own needs' (WCED, 1987, 8).

Many argue that sustainable development has become the 'dominant paradigm' when considering how to respond to environmental change

Table 1.2: The development of environmental policy at the EU level

Year	Event
1972	EU environmental policy was formally founded through the European Council declaration made in Paris in October 1972.
1972	The EU adopts its first Environment Action Programme, based on the ideas that prevention is better than cure and the 'polluter pays' principle. The first environment ministries are established.
1975	The Community starts building its body of environmental legislation with the adoption of – among others – the Waste Framework Directive (1975), the Bathing Water Directive (1976) and the Birds Directive (1979).
1980+	The EU continues to build the main body of its environmental legislation with the adoption of key pieces of legislation such as the Environmental Impact Assessment Directive (1985). The German Green Party is founded, and enters parliament for the first time in 1983.
1987	The Single European Act incorporates environmental protection into the Treaty of Rome. The year is designated as the European Year of the Environment.
1990 +	Adoption of, among others, the Urban Waste Water Treatment Directive (1991), the Habitats Directive (1992), the Packaging and Packaging Waste Directive (1994), the Air Quality Framework Directive (1996), and the Integrated Pollution Prevention Control Directive (1996).
1992	At the UN summit on the environment and development in Rio de Janeiro, the Agenda 21 programme is adopted. The Community and its Member States sign the UN Framework Convention on Climate Change and the Convention on Biodiversity.
1992	The EU's 5th Environment Action Programme puts integration of environment into other policy areas at its core, signalling a shift from purely regulatory measures to an emphasis on economic and fiscal measures.
1998	The UNECE Convention on Access to Information, Public Participation in Decision-making and Access to Justice in Environmental Matters (the 'Aarhus Convention') is adopted at the Fourth Ministerial Conference in the 'Environment for Europe' process.

Year	Event
1999	The Amsterdam Treaty enters into force, requiring that environmental protection be integrated in the definition and implementation of Community policies and activities, with a view to promoting sustainable development.
2000 +	Adoption of the Water Framework Directive (2000), End-of-Life Vehicles Directive (2000), REACH – the Registration, Evaluation and Authorisation of Chemicals (2006) and Directive on 'Strategic Environmental Assessment' (2001).
	The European Commission issues the Biodiversity Action Plan, and launches its Clean Air for Europe programme.
	The European Council in Gothenburg results in a declaration 'A Sustainable Europe for a Better World: A European Strategy for Sustainable Development'.
2003	The EU Emissions Trading Scheme enters into effect, creating a market for carbon dioxide allowances
2007	IPCC report Climate Change 2007: The Physical Science Basis concludes that the proof of climate change is 'unequivocal'. Europe's leaders agree to adopt new targets to reduce carbon dioxide emissions by 20% from 1990 levels by 2020.

Source: Adapted from European Environment Agency, 2013

(see Langhelle, 2000; Baker, 2006; Redclift, 2005). Indeed, Redclift (2005, 212) suggests that the 1987 Brundtland report led 'directly to the term ... passing into policy discourse, if not into everyday language'. The concept of sustainable development has also become embedded in the institutions responsible for environment and development policy at all scales. The term appears in international conventions and strategies, government strategy documents, local and national plans. As Ratner (2004, 50) suggests, 'the ideal of sustainable development retains currency across a remarkably broad swath of the political spectrum in debating alternative scenarios for the future'. However, sustainable development has been criticised for unnecessarily complicating the discussion of environmental issues, for being too anthropocentric, and for being too optimistic in assuming that all environment and development problems have win/win solutions (Meadowcroft, 2000). On the other hand, its strengths lie in 'its focus on global issues, on linking economic and environmental decision-making, on inter- and intra-generational equity, and on achieving structural reform while leaving it open to experience to establish the ultimate parameters of the required change' (Meadowcroft, 2000, 384). What is important about the use of the term sustainable development is that it reflects a global shift away from the 'traditional model of environmental policy' (Carter, 2007, 211). Instead of a piecemeal and non-strategic approach to environmental policy centred on techno-centric end-of-pipe solutions, sustainable development has provided the possibility for strategic and holistic policy making that recognises the importance of the relationship between society and the environment.

Baker (2006) suggests that within international policy debates the term sustainable development has been associated with six normative principles. These have been defined by Baker (2006, 36) as 'moral statements that specify what is good or bad and mould attitudes and guide behaviour'. They include common but differentiated responsibilities, inter- and intra-generational equity, justice, participation, and gender equality. It is these principles that underlie many international policy debates (see Table 1.3).

In addition to these, there are two further elements that are implicit within Baker's six normative principles: policy integration and planning and the precautionary principle. Policy integration and planning refer largely to the institutions and processes associated with environmental policy making. As described above, environmental policies have been traditionally piecemeal and fragmented, with most action typically taking place in specific environmental departments. Many have argued that to achieve more positive policy outcomes, governmental departments need to broaden their working patterns and focus, integrating environmental concerns into their day to day business, and working more closely with others with similar policy goals, reforming and adapting where necessary (Carter, 2007). Planning suggests that policy goals need to be thought out and delivered appropriately, using a range of policy levels and policy instruments (Carter, 2007).

The precautionary principle is based around three core elements; first, that there is a possible hazard to the environment, second, that the levels of risk and possible outcomes are uncertain, and third, that

Table 1.3: Baker's normative principles of sustainable development

Normative principles	Description
Common but differentiated responsibilities	Considering both the varying negative effects that different countries have had on the environment over time and space, and different countries' ability to act within policy responses.
Inter-generational equity	Equity between generations – this is handled explicitly in the Brundtland report, and considers the long term consequences of existing patterns of consumption and pollution.
Intra generational equity Justice	Equity and justice within our own generation – considering issues such as the global north/south divide, relationships between poverty and the causes and effects of environmental degradation. Environmental justice debates fall under this heading, as do issues around adaption to environmental problems.
Participation	Participation tends to encourage the involvement of the citizenry in decision-making (see Chapter 3). This is based on ideas of democratic decision-making (rather than imposing decisions in a top down manner). It is also suggested that participation promotes environmental education, a greater understanding about the need to make 'difficult' decisions, and better policy through the integration of lay knowledge.
Gender equality	This dimension considers that environmental problems may affect men and women differently, and that societal roles can be divided along gender lines.

Source: Baker, 2006, 36–47

there is a course of action that can be taken to eliminate or reduce the possible but uncertain risk (Turner and Hartzell, 2004). The precautionary principle has become mainstream in environmental thought following its description in Agenda 21 as 'a lack of full scientific certainty shall not be used as a reason for postponing cost-effective measures to prevent environmental degradation' (UNCED, 1992b). However, the extent to which the principle is employed in policy making is debatable, and varies by sector and environmental issue.

Thinking about policy responses: ecological modernisation

Ecological modernisation is an alternative paradigm that has emerged in response to the difficulties of putting sustainable development principles into practice. Rather than requiring a radical shift in the attitudes and behaviours of government, business and society, ecological modernisation attempts to reform current institutions to make them more 'environmentally friendly'. Ecological modernisation provides for the possibility that profits can be made while protecting the environment. There are important differences between ecological modernisation and sustainable development. While sustainable development has at its core issues of ecology, social justice and global concerns, ecological modernisation focuses on the internalisation of environmental problems into existing economic, political and social systems. As Langhelle (2000, 318) points out: 'At best, ecological modernisation is a "weak" expression of sustainable development. It should be seen as a necessary, but not sufficient condition for sustainable development'. There are two major assumptions that are made by proponents of ecological modernisation:

1. Science and technology are central to solutions for environmental problems. Technology can deliver at all points in the manufacturing process; in reducing the demands on resources, controlling pollution, and reducing waste by encouraging re-use and recycling. These controls not only benefit the environment but also improve efficiency and reduce costs for business.
2. 'The market plays a central role in the transmission of ecological ideas and practices' (Carter, 2007, 228). Growing markets in green technologies, and green consumerism, increases the demand for goods and services which minimise their impact on the environment. By internalising external environmental costs through the application of market-based instruments such as eco-taxes the market also becomes more efficient as a means of resource allocation and decision-making).

The suggested benefits of ecological modernisation lie in its ability to engage with the business sector. As Carter (2007, 229) puts it, 'ecological modernisation appeals to business in a language it understands – profit – which makes it more likely that business will be won over'. It also offers a clear set of policies that can be practically implemented, whereas sustainable development presents difficulties in implementation, particularly in matters of inequality and social justice.

Scope of *The short guide to environmental policy*

This short guide focuses on the need for environmental policies, and how these are formulated and implemented. As such there are several notable omissions; alternative green perspectives, and closely related, a detailed study of social movements and direct action.

Eco anarchist, deep ecologist, eco socialist, and eco feminist approaches (to name just a few) offer different perspectives regarding the nature of the environment and the human–environment relationship, and often question existing social, economic and policy norms. While these perspectives provide an interesting insight into debates around the ambition and effectiveness of current policies, whether they have substantially influenced policy within liberal democracies is perhaps questionable (Carter, 2007) and it is beyond the scope of this guide to consider this.

Additionally, the role of social movements and direct action – that is, action that challenges or attempts to prevent policy through forms of protest – are not considered within this text. Direct action may be taken for a range of reasons, to raise public and political awareness about an issue, to protest against a decision or action, or to prevent a course of action taking place. In the words of one protester: '[we] tried to use the democratic processes…[but] the government isn't listening' (BBC, 2013). While this statement, and indeed these forms of protest offer an insight into criticisms of existing policy and indeed, sometimes influence policy both directly or indirectly (see Chapters Four and Five), it is beyond the scope of the guide to consider the nature and politics of direct action.

Further reading for these subjects is suggested in the reading guide.

How to use this book

Having introduced how the environment has become a prominent issue of concern over the past half century, and briefly outlined key policy responses, the rest of this short guide considers the complexities of the human–environment relationship, theoretical perspectives about this relationship, styles of policy making, barriers to policy making, and the key challenges facing policy makers over the next three decades.

Chapter Two provides an overview of current key environmental problems, their causes and effects. It highlights the main challenges for policy makers, that is, to limit environmental damage and unequal impacts, and to balance development needs. Chapter Three explores different theoretical perspectives that often underpin societal understanding of environmental problems and subsequent policy responses – most notably those grounded in sociology, economics and social policy. Chapter Four considers the development of environmental policy, and outlines how policy debates have emerged and developed since the 1960s. It outlines the key policy instruments available to policy makers including market-based instruments, regulation and education/information campaigns. Chapter Five evaluates policy progress, considering barriers, limitations and failings of environmental policies. Chapter Six concludes by considering the key challenges facing environmental policy makers over the coming decades, particularly resource depletion, climate change and the food, water, energy nexus.

SUMMARY

- Some argue that the rate and scale of human-induced global environmental change now constitutes a new geological epoch in the Earth's history called the Anthropocene.
- Over the last 60 years modern environmental awareness has increased with the emergence of each new environmental issue.
- Media coverage of dramatic pollution events, green activism, political green movements, influential publications and new institutions to campaign for and protect the environment have all influenced our awareness and understanding of the importance of the environment for human survival.
- As knowledge and thinking about the environment changed, global responses to environmental challenges have developed.
- Since the publication of the Brundtland Report, *Our common future* (WCED, 1987), the term 'sustainable development' has become commonplace within policy circles.

READING GUIDE

Baker, S, 2006, *Sustainable development*, London: Routledge

Blewitt, J, 2008, Understanding sustainable development, London: Earthscan

Carter, N, 2007, *The politics of the environment*, 2nd edn, Cambridge: Cambridge University Press

Haq, G, Paul, A, 2012, *Environmentalism since 1945*, London: Routledge

Hayes, S, 2000, A history of environmental politics since 1945, Pittsburgh, PA: University of Pittsburgh Press

IISD (International Institute for Sustainable Development), 2013, What is sustainable development, www.iisd.org/sd/

McNeil, JR, 2000, So*mething new under the sun: an environmental history of the world in the 20th century*, Cambridge: Cambridge University Press

UNEP (United Nations Environment Programme) , www.unep.org/

WCED (World Commission on Environment and Development), 1987, *Our common future,* (Bruntland report), Oxford: Oxford University Press

Further reading on green perspectives and movements

Carter, N, 2007, *The politics of the environment*, 2nd edn, Cambridge: Cambridge University Press (chs 2 and 3 in 'Thinking about the environment')

Dobson, A, 2007, *Green political thought*, 4th edn, London: Routledge

Dobson, A, Eckersley, R, 2006, *Political theory and the ecological challenge* Cambridge: Cambridge University Press

Liddick, DR, 2006, Eco-terrorism, radical environmental and animal liberation movements, Westport, CT: Praeger

St Clair, J, Frank, J, 2013, *The Green fuse: Inside the radical environmental movement*, Oakland, CA: AK Press

2

Causes and effects of current environmental problems

Introduction

The DPSIR (drivers–pressures–state–impacts–responses) conceptual framework allows an understanding of the relationship between the drivers of human development, pressures on the environment and resulting social and environmental impacts (see Figure 2.1). *Drivers* are social, economic or environmental developments and include population growth and economic development. Different aspects of these drivers can exert particular *pressures* on the environment via

Figure 2.1: DPSIR conceptual framework

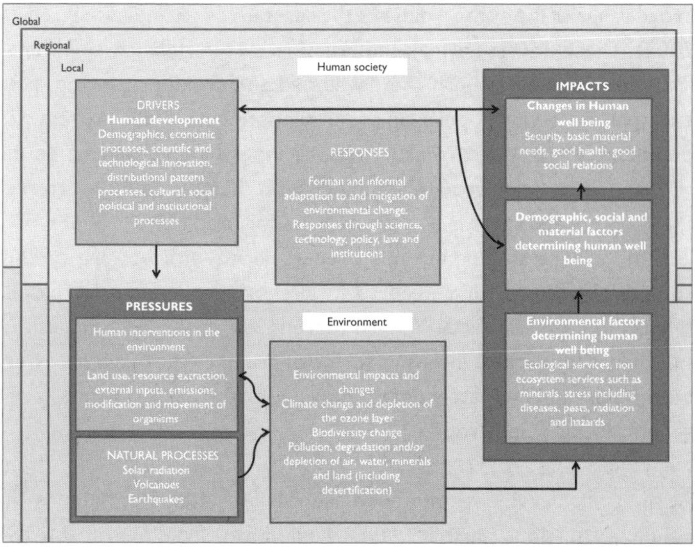

transport, urbanisation and globalisation (UNEP, 2011). These *pressures* can result in a change in the *state* of the environment, which leads to an *impact* (social, economic and environmental). The *impact* can cause public and political concern which results in a societal *response* which can feed back and affect other parts of the framework.

This chapter uses the DPSIR framework to consider the different dimensions of the human–environment relationship and how these issues translate into specific environmental policy challenges.

Drivers, pressures and natural processes

Over the past 150 years increasing industrialisation, motorisation, urbanisation and rapid social change have led to environmental degradation. Technological developments have resulted in the widespread availability of goods and services now considered to be integral to our daily lives. These include the availability of energy, clean water, private transport and access to the internet and to a broad range of foods regardless of the season (for example, see Cahill, 2002). These drivers have placed pressure on the global, national and local environment in both the developed and developing world. For example, increasing population and urbanisation have placed pressure on undeveloped land such as forests, or indeed arable land (Zhao et al, 2009). Population growth combined with changing dietary patterns are likely to lead to an increased demand for food (FAO, 2006; FAO, 2012b). Where arable land has been replaced with housing or for commercial use this may lead to food shortages, and an increased reliance on food imports. Where there is less space for agriculture, this may lead to more intensive forms of farming that result in lower crop yields, and ultimately desertification, or the use of chemicals or genetically modified crops.

At the global level, environmental changes are often associated with polluting emissions (in solid, gas or liquid form) from human activity and the destruction of natural resources. It is argued by some that globalisation has intensified environmental change (for example, see Tisdell, 2001). Global markets and the demand for goods and services mean that activities in one country have environmental implications in other countries. Globalisation has effectively reduced the distances between social actors with new forms of communication linking consumers to the environments in other parts of the world. For example, European demand for hardwoods used in furniture construction has driven large-scale deforestation in parts of South America such as the Amazon rainforest. Deforestation not only has local consequences in terms of the loss of biodiversity and environmental quality in Latin America, but the loss of ecosystem services that these forests provide, as a natural sink for carbon dioxide, which has global consequences. This shift in production and consumption has led to increased global trade and changes in consumer habits – for example, an expectation for low cost clothes and certain food products to be available throughout the year (Nerlich and Lien, 2004).

Technological changes have enabled this shift in production and consumption. For example, the rise of aviation and air freight have enabled the rapid distribution of goods (Docherty and Shaw, 2008). Equally, the internet, mobile technology and computing have led to a more connected population that is able to shop internationally without leaving the home. This advance in technology, together with economic growth, has led to a highly mobile and fast-moving society and a boom of consumerism in the West. Similar trends are also observable in rapidly developing economies, where the desire for both essential goods and services and luxury goods is increasing. While such developments are in many respects beneficial for a proportion of the population, these can still have detrimental environmental and social effects.

In addition to this, the imperative to meet basic human needs can also be associated with environmental damage, with the Brundtland report suggesting that 'Those who are poor and hungry will often destroy their immediate environment in order to survive' (WCED, 1987, 28). Equally, natural environmental processes also require recognition, these are beyond human intervention but may put significant pressure on the environment. The most notable processes include volcanoes and earthquakes, with the former having a significant impact on local environments.

Environmental Impacts and change

Table 2.1 provides a list of key human activities, their outputs, and consequent environmental impacts. The environmental impact from human activity combined with natural events can result in environmental change that affects atmosphere, land, water and biodiversity.

Atmosphere

Climate change is regarded by many as one of the greatest threats to human security (UNFCCC, 2012b). Box 2.1 summarises the key drivers and effects of climate change. While there has been significant and substantial debate regarding climate science, there is a scientific consensus that human activities are causing changes in the global climate system (IPCC, 2007b). One area of uncertainty however and something that makes policy so difficult, is knowing future effects and trends (Schneider et al, 2010).

Ozone depletion is also regarded as a significant environmental problem, although it is often discussed in environmental policy terms as an area of policy success, where policy interventions have substantially prevented further damage (UNEP, 2012; Carter, 2007), with some models suggesting that without policy intervention there would have been an increase in ultraviolet (UV) radiation of 300 per cent (UNEP, 2012, 52). Box 2.2 highlights the importance of the ozone layer to human health, and indicates how it became depleted.

In addition to climate change and ozone depletion, there are many other forms (that is, indoor, outdoor, regional and transboundary) of air pollution that result from human activities. Outdoor air pollution is among one of the most important environmental risk factors for human health. An estimated 2.1 million people die globally each year

Table 2.1: Human activities, outputs, environmental changes

Human activities	Water consumption
	Food production and consumption
	Domestic energy production and consumption
	Creation and maintenance of infrastructure
	Transport
	Industrial processes
	Waste disposal
	Housing construction
	Leisure activities (e.g long-haul flights)
Outputs from these activities	Pesticides/herbicides
	Greenhouse gases
	Lead/heavy metals
	Polyvinyl chloride (PVC)/Halogen compounds
	Dioxins
	Municipal waste
	Industrial toxic waste
	Industrial other waste
	Trade effluents
	Sewage
	Chloroflurocarbons (CFCs) and other ozone depleters
	Resource depletion
Consequent environmental problems	Landscape degradation
	Land subsidence
	Flooding
	Desertification
	Soil deterioration
	Water pollution
	Land pollution
	Air pollution
	Climate change
	Acid deposition
	Ozone depletion
	Radioactivity
	Loss of biodiversity

Source: Snell, 2009 adapted from Huby, 1998

Box 2.1: Climate change: the basics

It is now well-established that the:

- concentration of greenhouse gases in the Earth's atmosphere is directly linked to the average global temperature on Earth;
- concentration of greenhouse gases has been rising steadily together with mean global temperatures since the time of the Industrial Revolution; and
- the most abundant greenhouse gas, carbon dioxide, is the product of burning fossil fuels.

Greenhouse gases occur naturally and are responsible for keeping some of the sun's warmth from reflecting back into space and making Earth liveable. This is essential for human survival and the survival millions of other living things. However, industrialisation, destruction of forests and intensive farming methods have driven up quantities of greenhouse gases in the atmosphere.

The average temperature of the Earth's surface has risen by 0.74°C since the late 1800s. If no action is taken, average global temperature is expected increase by another 1.8°C to 4°C by the year 2100. That's a fast and intense change in geological time. Even if it 'only' gets another 1.8°C hotter, it would be a larger increase in temperature than any century-long trend in the last 10,000 years.

- Approximately 20–30 per cent of plant and animal species is likely to be at higher risk of extinction if the global average temperature goes up by more than 1.5 to 2.5°C.
- Nine of the last ten years were the hottest years on record, according to the United States' National Oceanic and Atmospheric Administration (NOAA). The years 2005 and 2010 tied for first place; in second place was 1998.
- The average sea level rose by 10 to 20 cm over the twentieth century. An additional increase of 18 to 59 cm is expected

by the year 2100. Higher temperatures cause ocean volume to expand. Melting glaciers and ice caps add more water. And as the bright white of ice and snow give way to dark sea green, fewer and fewer rays from the sun are reflected back into space, intensifying the heating.

(Adapted from UNFCCC, 2013)

Box 2.2: Ozone

Stratospheric ozone protects humans and other organisms because it absorbs UV-B radiation from the sun. In humans, heightened exposure to UV-B radiation increases the risk of skin cancer, cataracts and suppression of the immune system. Excessive UV-B exposure can also damage terrestrial plant life, single-cell organisms and aquatic ecosystems. In the mid-1970s, it was discovered that the thinning of the stratospheric ozone layer was linked to the steady increase of CFCs – used for refrigeration and air conditioning, foam blowing and industrial cleaning – in the atmosphere. The most severe and surprising ozone loss – which came to be known as the ozone hole – was discovered to be recurring in springtime over the Antarctic. Thinning of the ozone layer has also been observed over other regions, such as the Arctic (Manney et al, 2011) and northern and southern mid-latitudes.

(UNEP, 2012, 51)

due to inhaling fine particulate matter ($PM_{2.5}$) emitted by diesel engines, power plants and coal fires. Another 470,000 are thought to die due to high levels of ground-level ozone, created when vehicle exhaust gases react with oxygen (Silva et al, 2013). Many deaths due to outdoor air pollution are estimated to occur in the major and mega cities in East and South Asia, where population is high and air pollution is severe (Schwela et al, 2006). For example, China has gone through a period of rapid economic growth and urbanisation over the last three decades.

Sulphur dioxide (SO_2) from coal burning was found to exceed national environmental standards, and was linked to acid rain in 38 per cent of the country's cities (Chan and Yao, 2008). While the emissions of some air pollutants have begun to decrease in China, there are still levels of ground-level ozone (O_3) and particulate matter ($PM_{2.5}$ and PM_{10}) that are well above World Health Organization (WHO) air quality guidelines (Chan and Yao, 2008). Not only do these pollutants have negative environmental effects (such as damage to biodiversity), they are also associated with damage to crops, buildings and human health and wellbeing.

Land

Land degradation, desertification and pollution are all changes that have occurred as a result of human activities. Typically, human drivers of land degradation relate to over-cultivation, over-grazing, deforestation and urbanisation. According to UNEP, there are a number of interrelated issues associated with land degradation:

- increased intensive farming
- increased demands on land resources
- urbanisation and migration (with half the world's population living in cities)
- unsustainable land use
- land degradation in the form of soil erosion, nutrient depletion and water scarcity
- desertification
- threats to forestry.

As well as the release of harmful and persistent pollutants (heavy metals, organic chemicals) associated with mining, manufacturing, sewage, energy and transport emissions, agrochemicals, and stockpiles of obsolete chemicals (UNEP, 2007, 82–3), an increased demand for housing, infrastructure, industry, energy-intensive food production and the need to feed 7 billion people have all placed a pressure on land (FAO, 2006; UN, 2012). Urban expansion has encroached on to prime agricultural land resulting in poorer quality land being brought into cultivation (Dyson, 1996). However, in order to feed a burgeoning population greater crop productivity will be required. According to the FAO, 'In 1960, the average hectare of arable land, globally, supported 2.4 persons. By 2005 this figure had increased to 4.5 persons per hectare and by 2050 the estimate is that a hectare of land will have to support between 6.1 and 6.4 people' (FAO, 2009). Each hectare of land will need to produce more food to meet demand which may require the adoption of intensive farming processes. Such processes can be environmentally damaging and result in poor crop productivity (FAO, 2009). Land degradation may also lead to desertification in arid, semi-arid and dry sub-humid areas again reducing food production, exhausting water supplies, increasing water- and food-borne diseases due to poor hygiene and limited clean water and eventually leading to population displacement (UNCED, 1992b; WHO, 2013b). These pressures will be exacerbated by climate change which will ultimately threaten food security (FAO, 2012a).

Land can be further degraded by deforestation. This has local and global impacts. At the global level, forests act as a natural 'carbon sink' which if destroyed reduces the Earth's natural capacity to absorb carbon dioxide, which will affect the pace of climate change. In addition, forests support biodiversity and provide 'ecosystem services' such as preventing soil erosion, maintaining soil fertility and protecting water catchments. Forestry provides economic benefits and supports industries such as timber, pulp and biotechnology (UNEP, 2007; Forestry Commission, 2013).

Land pollution includes chemical contamination, which is where land is exposed to chemicals such as DDT, lead, toxic substances such as cyanide and mercury (UNEP, 2007, 94). Industry, agriculture and municipalities can release chemicals that can affect the local environment or be deposited elsewhere via air or water. In addition, the disposal of toxic or hazardous waste can also pose a threat to human health and remain contaminated for long periods (UNEP, 2007, 94–5).

Water

UNEP's GEO5 assessment of the state of the global environment highlighted water sources as being highly vulnerable to pollution:

> As the ultimate sink for pollutants, freshwater and marine ecosystems are among the most sensitive indicators of the environmental impacts of human activities. They support a wide diversity of life, providing important goods and services that directly or indirectly support and sustain human existence and livelihoods. Adequate freshwater supplies of acceptable quality are recognized as a human right by the UN General Assembly's declaration on clean water and sanitation. (UNEP, 2012, 100)

An estimated 70 per cent of marine pollution is caused by land based activities, with only an additional 10 per cent (each) caused by maritime transport and dumping at sea activities (UNCED, 1992, 150; 2012b). Equally, fresh water sources are susceptible to many forms of pollution. Pollution from industry, agriculture, transport, and waste are all possible sources of fresh water contamination. One common problem associated with human or animal waste and fertilisers entering water systems is eutrophication (that is, excess nutrients that stimulate plant growth). This can damage biodiversity, threaten coastal ecosystems and may have detrimental effects on the food chain and human health (for example, through paralytic shellfish poison, or the reduction of fisheries resources) (UNEP, 2012, 112).

Biodiversity

Biological diversity also known as biodiversity refers to diversity within the living world (UNEP and WCMC, 2013). While some argue that biodiversity has inherent value, many others highlight the importance of biodiversity to human wellbeing. The UK's Department for Environment and Rural Affairs (Defra) describes biodiversity as 'supporting the ecological services that humans require to live' (Defra, 2011, 3). Biodiversity is often seen as the 'building blocks' of ecosystems. Ecosystems provide a range of services for human wellbeing including fresh air, water, and food. The main threats to biodiversity are thought to be 'habitat loss and degradation from agriculture and infrastructure development, overexploitation, pollution and invasive alien species' (UNEP, 2012, 134).

Human activities also threaten species, and in some cases cause extinction. For example, in 2012, the IUCN red list which provides which taxonomic, conservation status and distribution information on plants and animals updated its current list of threatened species. (IUCN, 2012) (see Table 2.2). Table 2.2 demonstrates how the number of 'critically endangered species' have increased significantly since 1996. The loss of species represents both a loss of a unique form of life, and also has negative implications for human wellbeing.

Table 2.2: IUCN list of critically endangered species in 2012

Year	Mammals	Birds	Reptiles	Amphibians	Fish	Insects	Molluscs	Plants
1996/98	169	168	41	18	157	44	257	909
2000	180	182	56	25	156	45	222	1,014
2002	181	182	55	30	157	46	222	1,046
2003	184	182	57	30	162	46	250	1,276
2004	162	179	64	413	171	47	265	1,490
2006	162	181	73	442	253	68	265	1,541
2007	163	189	79	441	254	69	268	1,569
2008	188	190	86	475	289	70	268	1,575
2009	188	192	93	484	306	89	291	1,577
2010	188	190	106	486	376	89	373	1,619
2011	194	189	137	498	414	91	487	1,731
2012	196	197	144	509	415	119	549	1,821

Source: IUCN, 2012

Human dimensions

A number of environmental threats affect human health and wellbeing. These can be naturally occurring environmental threats or human-induced environmental threats. It is often the old, poor and young who are more vulnerable to the effects of environmental change. As a consequence, these groups tend to be disproportionately affected, with environmental inequalities existing at the local, national and international level in both the developed and developing world.

Basic material needs: food, water, shelter

Environmental change often threatens the fulfilment of basic human needs such as food, water and shelter. The UN Millennium Development Goals (MGD) highlight the importance of a safe water supply:

■ Every day, 2 million tons of sewage and other effluents drain into the world's waters.
■ Every year, more people die from unsafe water than from all forms of violence, including war.
■ The most significant sources of water pollution are lack of inadequate treatment of human wastes and inadequately managed and treated industrial and agricultural wastes. (UN, 2013)

Increased water extraction, deforestation and desertification may reduce water quality and availability. Inadequate water supply is considered to be an regional issue as it is dependent on 'basin-level water scarcity, regional water quality, inadequacies of infrastructure and governance, cultural perspectives and inequitable water pricing' (UNEP, 2012, 114). As well as water scarcity, flooding and drought also impact on human health and wellbeing. While these are naturally occurring events, climate change is expected to increase the frequency of extreme weather with floods and droughts being responsible for billions of dollars of damage each year. 'Climate change is altering the hydrologic cycle, threatening freshwater and marine ecosystems as well as human water security in many regions' (UNEP, 2012, 98–9). The Japan tsunami (see Box 2.3) and the Bangladesh floods (see Box 2.4) illustrate how both the developed and developing world are being affected by natural environmental threats.

Box 2.3: *Japan Daily Press* article about the 2011 tsunami

It's been 18 months since the devastating earthquake and tsunami hit Japan and the grim fact remains – around three thousand people are still missing. Tuesday marked the one and a half year anniversary and a sad reminder of the 15,870 people who died in the chaos. Hard facts are that more than 343,000 people living in about 136,000 temporary homes. This includes provisional housing and private properties rented by the government. The police and Japan Coast Guard officers in disaster-hit areas of Iwate, Miyagi and Fukushima prefectures are still on the lookout for the missing persons and have deployed around 800 people for the same. Although hopes of finding survivors are bleak, all that they can find are the remains of those who succumbed to that fateful day in March. If we go by the prefectural numbers then 1,205 in Iwate, 1,426 in Miyagi and 211 in Fukushima are still missing.

(*Japan Daily Press*, 2012)

Box 2.4: Bangladesh and natural hazards

Bangladesh is the ninth largest country in the world by population (164.4 million people) and is one of the most densely populated. Almost half of its 164.4 million people live on less than US$1.25 a day (World Bank, 2005) and 80 per cent on less than US$2.00 a day (DFID, 2011). The size and density of the population, together with regular extreme weather events, such as floods and cyclones, make the country extremely vulnerable to natural hazards becoming natural disasters. During the last ten years, 12 major natural disasters have afffected millions of people in Bangladesh, including floods in 2004, which affected 36 million people, and Cyclone Sidr in 2007, which affected over nine million people. Since 2000, US$430 million has been

> raised for disaster response with over half of it allocated to the
> humanitarian operation following Cyclone Sidr.
> (Global Humanitarian Assistance, 2012, 3)

Roberts and Parks (2007) suggest that some countries (and indeed communities within these countries) are more vulnerable to the effects of these events than others. They outline five main predictors of 'suffering' (vulnerability): 'the percentage of the population living in cities (safer), the percentage of the population living near a coast, high income inequality, a weak civil society, and nations with weak property rights regimes' (2007, 215). Developing countries may not always have the capacity to react or plan for environmental events, many have larger populations living in high risk areas, have fewer early warning systems and defence systems, and less capacity to act following an event (Ahmed et al, 2009). This is illustrated by comparing the ability of the Netherlands and Bangladesh to deal with tidal flooding (UNDP, 2008). While both are low-lying countries, the Netherlands has numerous defences, and in places, housing stock that rises with flood waters. It also has a strong civil society, and the capacity to recover from flooding. In contrast, Bangladesh does not have these mechanisms in place, has a higher proportion of people living flood risk areas, and high dependency on subsistence farming. Comparatively, the social cost of flooding (both in terms of mortality and morbidity) in Bangladesh is far higher than it is in the Netherlands.

Natural disasters also threaten food security, especially in developing countries where there is a greater reliance on subsistence farming. The World Food Programme states that 'In purely quantitative terms, there is enough food available to feed the entire global population of 7 billion people. And yet, one out of every eight people is going hungry. One in three children is underweight' (WFP, 2013a). Climate change is expected to further exacerbate food security (see Box 2.5).

Box 2.5: Food security and climate change

Natural disasters such as floods, tropical storms and long periods of drought are on the increase with serious consequences for food security in developing countries. Drought is now the single most common cause of food shortages in the world. In 2006, recurrent drought caused crop failures and heavy livestock losses in parts of Ethiopia, Somalia and Kenya. In many countries, climate change is exacerbating already adverse natural conditions. For example, poor farmers in Ethiopia or Guatemala traditionally deal with rain failure by selling off livestock to cover their losses and pay for food. But successive years of drought, increasingly common in the Horn of Africa and Central America, are exhausting their resources.

(World Food Programme, 2013a)

Due to a combination of adverse agro-climatic, socio-economic and technological conditions, climate change is expected to affect 'crop production mainly in low latitude developing countries followed by mid- to high-latitude developed countries' (UNEP, 2007, 5.4.2). Table 2.3 highlights the regional affects climate change will have on food security in Africa and Asia.

Health

Both natural and human-induced environmental change can directly harm human health; for example, via poor urban air quality or indirectly such as the increase of skin cancer due to ozone depletion (Slaper et al, 1996). The negative health impacts associated with exposure to certain pollutants are well documented (see, for example, WHO, 2013a). For example, many developed countries have introduced air quality guidelines and limits to improve urban air quality and have banned leaded petrol. Environmental hazards are responsible for approximately a quarter of the total burden of disease worldwide (WHO, 2010). In regions such as Sub-Saharan African it is responsible for as much as 30

Table 2.3: Specific climatic impacts on food security (Africa and Asia)

Africa	Asia
Increased vulnerability to climate change due to dependence on rain fed agriculture, high levels of poverty, low levels of human and physical capital as well as a predominately poor infrastructure. By 2050 crop yields in Sub-Saharan Africa will have declined by 14 per cent (rice), 22 per cent (wheat) and 5 per cent (maize) pushing the vast number of already poor, who depends on agriculture for their livelihoods, deeper into poverty and vulnerability. Decreased food availability by 500 calories less per person in 2050 – a 21 per cent decline. A further increase in the number of malnourished children by over 10 million – a total of 52 million in 2050 in Sub-Saharan Africa alone.	The Asia region will experience up to 50 per cent decline (wheat) and 17 per cent (rice) in crop yields by 2050 compared to 2000 levels. Decreasing yields threatens the food security for over 1.6 billion people. A significant negative impact on progress made reducing the proportion of malnourished children, increasing the number by about 11 million in comparison with a no climate change scenario. Asia accounts for 89 per cent of people affected by disasters worldwide. About 60 per cent of the economically active population and their dependents – 2.2 billion people, rely on agriculture production for their livelihoods..

Source: World Food Programme, 2013b, 7

per cent. Approximately 13 million deaths could be prevented every year by improving environmental quality. The WHO list ten key facts and figures that relate to the environment and health:

1. Worldwide, 13 million deaths could be prevented every year by making our environments healthier.
2. In children under the age of five, one third of all disease is caused by environmental factors such as unsafe water and air pollution.
3. Every year, the lives of four million children aged under five years – mostly in developing countries – could be saved by preventing environmental risks such as unsafe water and polluted air.

4. In developing countries, the main environmentally caused diseases are diarrhoeal disease, lower respiratory infections, unintentional injuries and malaria.

5. Better environmental management could prevent 40 per cent of deaths from malaria, 41 per cent of deaths from lower respiratory infections, and 94 per cent of deaths from diarrhoeal disease – three of the world's biggest childhood killers.

6. In the least developed countries, one third of death and disease is a direct result of environmental causes.

7. In developed countries, healthier environments could significantly reduce the incidence of cancers, cardiovascular diseases, asthma, lower respiratory infections, musculoskeletal diseases, road traffic injuries, poisonings and drownings.

8. Environmental factors influence 85 out of the 102 categories of diseases and injuries listed in *The World Health Report*.

9. Much of this death, illness and disability could be prevented through well-targeted interventions such as promoting safe household water storage, better hygiene measures and the use of cleaner and safer fuels.

10. Other interventions that can make environments healthier include: increasing the safety of buildings; promoting safe, careful use and management of toxic substances at home and in the workplace; and better water resource management. (WHO, 2010)

While there is extensive literature in this field, here we provide three brief case studies to illustrate the relationship between health and the environment: transport in the UK, the prevalence of cholera, and the impacts of climate change.

CASE STUDY ONE

Climate change and health

The health implications of climate change are highly complex and often interconnected with other environment and poverty issues. Heat waves and flooding are climate-related events that can have a direct and indirect impact on human health. For example, changing patterns of life-threatening vector-borne diseases such as malaria and other existing and emerging infectious diseases are expected due to higher frequency of flooding (WHO, October 2012c). Changes in food and water supply can have indirect health impacts for example, WHO (2003) suggests that by 2030 malnutrition will increase significantly in the South-East Asian region. The distribution of climate-related deaths is unequal, with most occurring within southern developing countries with the highest proportion in Sub-Saharan Africa. Future projections of the threats to human health indicate that a greater burden of effects will be felt by developing countries (both due to geographical factors and as a result of capacity to act and respond). The WHO suggests that climate change will increase the numbers killed or injured in coastal floods, noting that 'while these proportional increases are similar in developed and developing regions, the baseline rates are much higher in developing countries' (WHO, 2003).

Figure 2.2 presents the 'disease burden' of climate change up until 2000. This considers both years of life lost due to premature death, and years of life lived with a disability.

Figure 2.2: Disease burden of climate change

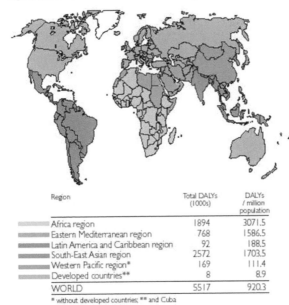

Region	Total DALYs (1000s)	DALYs / million population
Africa region	1894	3071.5
Eastern Mediterranean region	768	1586.5
Latin America and Caribbean region	92	188.5
South-East Asian region	2572	1703.5
Western Pacific region*	169	111.4
Developed countries**	8	8.9
WORLD	5517	920.3

* without developed countries; ** and Cuba

Source: WHO, 2003. Reproduced with the permission.

CASE STUDY TWO

Air pollution and ill health in the UK

There is a recognised link between various forms of air pollution and ill health, especially vehicle-related air pollution. Table 2.4 presents the main transport pollutants, sources and health impacts associated with UK road transport.

UK combustion emissions are responsible for an estimated 13,000 premature deaths with transport estimated to cause approximately 7,500 early deaths per year (Yim and Barrett, 2012, 1). The total monetized life loss in the UK is estimated at £6–£62 billion each year or 0.4–3.5 per cent of gross domestic product (Yim and Barrett, 2012, 1).

Table 2.4: Sources of pollution associated with transport and potential health effects

Pollutant	Main sources	From road transport in UK (%)	Possible health effects	Inequalities in exposure or susceptibility	C/ E/ D/ S
Benzene	Combustion and distribution of petrol	67	Genotoxic carcinogen, causes leukaemia	Those near petrol filling stations, Occupational exposure	C
1,3-Butadiene	Combustion of petrol	80	Genotoxic carcinogen, causes lymphomas and leukaemia		E
Carbon monoxide	Incomplete combustion	91	Increased deaths and Cardiovascular hospital admissions	*Harmful to those with pre-existing cardiovascular disease*	E
Nitrogen dioxide	Combustion in air: road transport, electrical supply industry, industry and commerce	46–61	Long-term: affects lung function, enhanced responses to allergens. Acute: as particulates	Unvented gas heaters, Gas cookers, Living near main roads *As particulates*	D E/S
Ozone	Sunlight acting on nitrogen oxides and volatile organic compounds	(Long distance pollutant)	Deaths and respiratory hospital admission Respiratory symptoms Lung function	Rural >Urban	E S
Particles	10: combustion (road traffic) 20: chemical reactions in air Coarse: for example, dust, soil, salt, pollen, tyres construction	25 higher in cities and in peak episodes	Acute: shortens lives, increases hospital admissions from respiratory and cardiovascular causes. Increased asthma symptoms and bronchodilator use	*Harmful to those with pre-existing cardiovascular or respiratory disease*	E D
Sulphur dioxide	Combustion of sulphur containing fuel	2	Respiratory and Cardio vascular deaths and respiratory hospital admissions brought forward Constriction of airways	Pre-existing asthma or chronic lung disease	E D

Note: CVD Cardiovascular, Each potential effect of transport on health is categorised below as Calculable (C), estimable (E), definite but unquantifiable (D), or speculative (S).

Source: Transport and Health Study Group, 2000

The British Medical Association suggest exposure to transport-related emissions can increase the risk of cardiovascular and respiratory disease, including heart attack and can affect physical development, increase the risk of mental illness and lead to poor school performance in children (BMA, 2012, 9). The negative health impacts associated with transport are disproportionately spread throughout the UK. The 2010 Marmot Review on UK health inequalities argues that those living in more socially deprived neighbourhoods are more likely to be presented with social and environmental risks to health. Poor air quality, a lack of green spaces and places for children to play, and greater risks from traffic are all highlighted as risks (Marmot Review Team, 2010, 78). Figure 2.3 presents the area of England with the 'least favourable' environmental conditions (including poor water and air quality, litter, flood risks) compared to those in the wealthiest areas.

Figure 2.3: Areas England and 'least favourable' environmental conditions

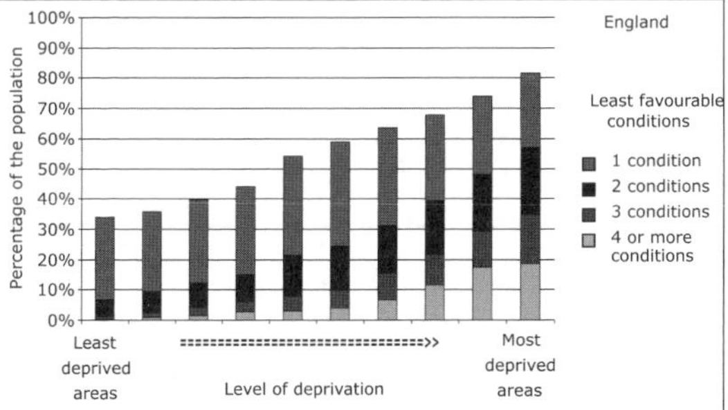

Note: Level of deprivation is determined by the Index of Multiple of Deprivation. Eleven environmental conditions or characteristics have been included: river water quality, air quality, green space, habitat favourable to biodiversity, flood risk, litter, housing conditions, road accidents, and presence of 'regulated sites' (e.g. waste management, industrial, or landfill sites, or sewage treatment works). For each of these conditions the population living in areas with, in relative terms, the 10 per cent least favourable conditions have been determined. Data range mainly from 2005 to 2008.

Source: Defra, Environment Agency, CLG

Source: Defra, 2013

As with many of the issues discussed so far, there are also risks associated with transport that are a result of human decisions, such as land use planning and social norms rather than the direct impacts of pollution. For example, evidence from the UK Department of Transport also highlights the number of people killed or seriously injured (KSI) by road transport between 2003 and 2012 (see Figure 2.4). While the KSI figure for car users has substantially reduced, cyclist injuries have increased, whereas motorcycle and pedestrian KSI numbers have reduced by a much smaller proportion in the same period. Overall, the data shows that 'vulnerable' road users (that is, pedestrians, cyclists and motorists) have a higher KSI rate than 'non vulnerable' road users (occupants of cars and other road users) (DfT, 2012, 2).

Figure 2.4: KSI statistics in the UK

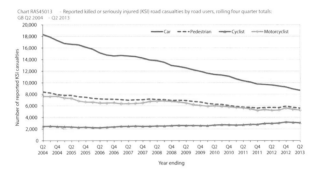

Note: The latest quarter data is provisional.
Source: DfT, 2012

CASE STUDY THREE

Impacts of poor water quality and sanitation – cholera

Cholera provides another example of both the negative human impacts of environmental change (for example, unsafe drinking water) *and* the impact of human factors such as urbanisation, overcrowding, poor infrastructure and hygiene practices. In 2000 Cholera was observed in 27 countries in Africa, nine in Latin American countries, 13 Asia, two in Europe and four in Oceania (WHO, 2012c) (see Box 2.6).

Box 2.6: Cholera: causes, effects and scope

Cholera is an acute infection of the intestine, which begins suddenly with painless watery diarrhoea, nausea and vomiting. Most people who become infected have very mild diarrhoea or symptom-free infection. Malnourished people in particular experience more severe symptoms. Severe cholera cases present with profuse diarrhoea and vomiting. Severe, untreated cholera can lead to rapid dehydration and death. If untreated, 50 per cent of people with severe cholera will die, but prompt and adequate treatment reduces this to less than one per cent of cases.

Cholera is caused by the bacterium *Vibrio cholerae*. People become infected after eating food or drinking water that has been contaminated by the faeces of infected persons. Raw or undercooked seafood may be a source of infection in areas where cholera is prevalent and sanitation is poor. Vegetables and fruit that have been washed with water contaminated by sewage may also transmit the infection if *V. cholerae* is present.

Control of cholera is a major problem in several Asian countries as well as in Africa. In the year 2000, some 140,000 cases resulting in approximately 5000 deaths were officially notified to WHO. Africa accounted for 87 per cent of these cases. After almost a century of no reported cases of the disease, cholera reached Latin America in 1991; however, the number of cases reported has been steadily declining since 1995.
(WHO, 2013a)

Cholera is often associated with untreated human or animal excrement. 'The vast majority of rivers in and around cities in developing countries are little more than open sewers and constitute a reservoir for cholera and other water-related diseases' (UNEP, 1997, 182). There is a close relationship between cholera and poverty, for example, the WHO identifies areas typically at risk of outbreaks as peri-urban slums with limited access to safe drinking water and lack of proper sanitation (WHO, 2012c). Figure 2.5 exaggerates a country's size according to the proportion of worldwide cholera deaths that have occurred there (where no deaths have occurred, the country is not present on the map). It is evident from the map that outbreaks are concentrated in poor, developing countries, mostly in Africa.

Figure 2.5: Cholera outbreaks

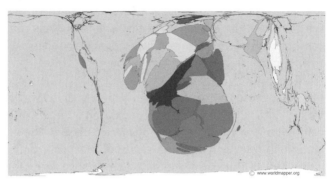

Source: Worldmapper.org, 2006
© Copyright Sasi Group (University of Sheffield) and Mark Newman
(University of Michigan)

Displaced populations are or those with no basic infrastructure are also at high risk of cholera. There is evidence to suggest that man-made or natural disasters may intensify epidemics (WHO, 2012a). WHO found that following the Rwandan genocide and subsequent population displacement cholera caused 23,800 deaths in one month in refugee camps in Goma (WHO, 2012b).

Security and social relations

Environmental changes can also threaten human security. For example, displacement and migration associated with environmental change and pollution have been well documented as populations attempt to move away from environmental hazards such as floods, volcanic eruptions, earthquakes, or severe pollution. It is suggested that climate change will exacerbate these problems, with some predicting that 'climate refugees' will increase by at least 50 million by 2050 (*National Geographic*, 2013).

There are also a number of serious threats to security as a result of environmental change. UNEP has listed 'Disasters and Conflicts' as one of its key areas of work, considering how resource scarcity may lead to conflict, but also how environmental disasters may have profound impacts on societies. Equally, it is suggested that conflict may degrade the natural environment and further limit access to essential resources such as food or water. The UNEP states 'As a victim or a driver of crisis, the environment can play a pivotal role in human security and well-being. Degraded or poorly managed ecosystems can lead to conflict over dwindling water, food or fuel resources, or to increased exposure and vulnerability to natural hazards such as landslides or flash floods' (UNEP, 2013, 1).

Over the past three decades, a number of conflicts have been associated with resources. For example, according to the UN 'the past half century has witnessed more than 500 conflict-related events over water, seven of which have involved violence' (UN, 2006). One particularly salient example is that of Darfur. Land degradation, deforestation, water scarcity, desertification along with additional pressures associated with climate change are all blamed in part for conflict in the region. Box 2.7 presents a summary of the UNEP's assessment of the conflict.

Box 2.7: UNEP's assessment of the Darfur conflict

Over the past four decades, the most serious concerns are land degradation, desertification and the spread of deserts southwards by an average of 100 km. These are linked with factors including over-grazing of fragile soils by a livestock population that has exploded from close to 27 million animals to around 135 million now.

Meanwhile, there is mounting evidence of long-term regional climate change in several parts of the country. This is witnessed by a very irregular but marked decline in rainfall, for which the clearest indications are found in Kordofan and Darfur states.

The scale of climate change as recorded in Northern Darfur is almost unprecedented, and its impacts are closely linked to conflict in the region, as desertification has added significantly to the stress on traditional agricultural and pastoral livelihoods. (UNEP, 2007)

Conclusions: the key policy challenges

This section consolidates some of the key themes discussed in this chapter, and highlights the key challenges for policy makers.

Balancing social, economic and environmental policy goals

A key policy challenge is ensuring an appropriate balance between social, economic and environmental policy goals. While many of the negative impacts discussed so far are linked to development and consumption, there is also a clear link between poverty, social deprivation and environmental problems. As is evident from the case studies presented here, environmental changes have disproportionate negative effects on human health and wellbeing. In wealthy countries such as the UK many environmental problems are caused by the consumption by wealthier sections of society, but are often felt disproportionately by poorer sections of society who are exposed 'environmental bads' without enjoying access to environmental 'goods' (see Chapter Three). Equally, at the international level, it is often action by developed countries that creates environmental problems for poorer countries. Referring to climate change, Roberts and Parks (2007, 7) argue that three interrelated forms of inequality exist at the global level: responsibility, vulnerability and adaptation. In terms of responsibility, developing countries have very low carbon emissions compared to developed countries. For example, Canadell et al (2009) found that from a historical perspective, developing countries with 80 per cent of the world's population still account for only 20 per cent of the cumulative emissions since 1751. The poorest countries in the world, with 800 million people, have contributed less than 1 per cent of these cumulative missions. However, in terms of the climate change effects, low lying developing countries or those in semi-arid areas face a greater proportion of floods and droughts compared to developed countries. They also have less political-economic capacity to prepare or respond to such events.

The challenge for policy makers is that attempts to improve the circumstances of the less well-off may (superficially at least) conflict with the need for environmental protection. For example, while addressing global hunger is clearly a vital development goal, the policy challenge is to improve food production and distribution without further environmental degradation.

Balancing uncertainty, risks and policy impacts

Appropriate policies must be adopted to protect economic, social or environmental needs. However, decision-making is often hampered by a lack of knowledge or certainty and whether the benefits of a policy measure outweigh the costs (see Chapters Three and Five). An example of this can be taken from the management of natural disasters. Box 2.8 presents a case study where a volcanic region was designated by policy makers as too dangerous for human habitation. However, those living in the area received many benefits from where they lived (including niche farming, strong community, and an indigenous way of life), and when policy makers decided to freeze any further physical or social infrastructure maintenance or development, the negative impacts on the communities were considered more damaging than the threat of the volcano.

Box 2.8: Volcanic risk management: getting the balance right

Volcanoes are commonly associated with violent eruptions, with the potential to destroy everything in their path. Yet even when faced with the potential loss of infrastructure, settlements, agriculture and even life, over 350 million people worldwide choose to live in close proximity to active volcanoes. Two predominant reasons given to justify this decision making are that people either lack understanding of the potential risks, or that their capacity to move elsewhere is constrained by their level of development. Less acknowledged is that many people choose to stay because of the benefits that the volcano provides to their livelihoods. Such benefits include:

- fertile soils for agriculture, enriched by volcanic ash
- abundant sources of fresh spring water used for drinking, washing, cooking and irrigation
- rocks and minerals, mined for construction
- forest products derived for building and fuel
- micro-climates, a product of topographical and altitudinal change used to grow a large variety of crops.

To limit potential loss, policy-makers need to ensure the protection of the population both before, during and after eruptions. Where policy can fail is in ensuring sustainability, often the result of failing to fully appreciate the relationship between the population and the volcano and the impact of separating one from the other. Strategies such as relocation and land zoning have the potential to be as detrimental to livelihoods as an eruption, resulting in homelessness, food insecurity, loss of agricultural land and job insecurity. Galeras, one of the most active volcanoes in Colombia (4276 m) reactivated in 1988, and has had continued activity with small predominantly ash style eruptions. In 2005 Galeras was declared a disaster zone, prohibiting any investment. This declaration has proved highly controversial due to the resultant interlocking web of social and economic impacts, including:

- water contamination due to aged aqueducts and pipe systems
- overcrowded housing due to prohibited new builds
- food insecurity due to lack of subsidies to help with rising costs of seeds, fertilisers and pesticides
- poor health as people can't afford to eat their home-grown fruit and vegetables, needing to sell them instead
- high unemployment due to lack of industry or other business investing

■　poor transport network due to unpaved roads.

The ongoing challenge for volcanic risk management lies in ensuring that policies both recognise and seek to support the value of volcanoes to the security and sustainability of their populations livelihoods, both for current and future generations. (*Written by Jessica Roberts*)

Scale

The case studies presented in this chapter have focused mainly on individual countries or regions. However, one key policy challenge is that environmental problems do not respect national or administrative boundaries. Pollution occurring in one country may have environmental effects elsewhere. Climate change is one example of this, where the effects of emissions largely attributed to developed countries are most likely to harm those in developing countries. Other examples include countries that share rivers and coast lines where pollution or over extraction from one country will affect another, or transboundary air pollution where the sources of air pollution emitted from one country have negative effects in another. Similar issues occur within countries, with local or regional forms of government often regarded as the most appropriate level of administration to ensure that an equal burden of environmental goods and bads are distributed nationally.

The key challenge here for environmental policy is to address environmental problems and their effects within this context. Clearly international level policy making is necessary in order to address global level issues, especially where the problem is caused by a multitude of countries. Equally, national, regional and local forms of decision-making are also important to ensure appropriate policy responses.

SUMMARY

- The natural environment provides human societies with a range of resources and services that are considered essential to human survival and development.
- The natural environment provides food, water and shelter, and also contributes to the regulation of air and water quality.
- The fulfilment of human needs results in environmental changes via the resource depletion, pollutant emissions and waste generation. Environmental changes include changes to the climate and ozone layer, biodiversity and pollution/degradation of land, water or air resources.
- Environmental change has a human cost and threatens the fulfilment of basic human needs such as access to food, water and shelter. This damages health and exacerbates conflict.
- Many of the human impacts on the environment are unequally distributed, with a burden often placed on older people, the young and those who are poor – both in the developing and the developed world. Equally, poverty may also exacerbate environmental problems.
- There are a number of environmental policy challenges: dealing with inequality and inequity; balancing environment and development; balancing uncertainty, risks and policy impacts; and assessing appropriate policy levels.

READING GUIDE

The human–environment relationship is a vast topic and readers are encouraged to examine the issues covered here in more detail elsewhere. Some of the most helpful literature can be accessed through organisations such as the UNEP, the WHO and IPCC. All have websites which are indicated below. In addition to these general sources a number of specific publications highlight a particular dimension of the human–environment relationship discussed in this chapter.

Chan, CK, Yao, X, 2008, Air pollution in mega cities in China, *Atmospheric Environment* 42, 1–42

Gouldie, A, 2006, The human impact on the natural environment: Past, present, and future, 6th edn, Oxford: Blackwell

Harper, C, 2007, Environment and society: Human perspectives on environmental issues, 4th edn, Pearson, New Jersey

IPCC (Intergovernmental Panel on Climate Change), 2007, *Climate Change 2007: Working Group II: Impacts, Adaptation and Vulnerability*, accessed at www.ipcc.ch/publications_and_data/ar4/wg2/en/ch5s5-4-2.html

UNCED (United Nations Conference on Environment and Development), 1992, *Agenda 21: The United Nations programme of action from Rio*, New York: United Nations

UNEP (United Nations Environment Programme), 2012, *Global environment outlook 5*, Nairobi: United Nations Environment Programme, www.unep.org/geo/geo5.asp

WHO (World Health Organization), 2003, *Climate change and human health: Risks and responses. Summary*, www.who.int/globalchange/publications/cchhsummary/en/index.html

Wilson, G, Furniss, P, Kimbowa, R (eds), 2008, *Environment, development, and sustainability: Perspectives and cases from around the world*, Oxford: Oxford University Press

3

Thinking about the environment

Introduction

There are many different ways of thinking about the human–environment relationship. At first glance some of the theoretical perspectives discussed in this chapter may appear rather removed from policy, however, when investigated in more depth, it becomes apparent that they help us to understand how environmental policies develop, how they are shaped, and why they might fail. This chapter begins by exploring economic perspectives about the environment. It considers the idea of negative environmental externalities, and recent attempts to put a value on environmental services and degradation. Sociological perspectives are then discussed, considering how understandings of environmental problems are embedded in society and culture. The relationship between science, technology and sociology is also explored, considering the objectivity of scientific evidence, and the importance of other types of evidence such as lay knowledge. Social policy perspectives are then outlined, considering issues of environmental (in)justice, and the 'greening' of institutions (as advocated by proponents of policy integration and ecological modernisation).

There are two notable omissions from this chapter. First, as discussed in Chapter One, while offering an interesting and insightful view into policy options that go beyond the mainstream, alternative political and philosophical perspectives regarding the environment are beyond the scope of this book. Second, political perspectives that consider the nature of environmental policy making and reasons for successes and failures are not considered here. Instead, as this is a large literature base, these perspectives are discussed in more detail in Chapters Four and Five.

Economic perspectives

Economic development has often been equated with progress driven by technological innovation. While capitalism and the quest for economic growth have produced many benefits they have been criticised for failing to reconcile the objectives of human development, poverty reduction and environmental sustainability. Economic development has come with a cost to the natural environment that is not reflected in the balance sheet. The expansion of the production of goods and services has required large amounts of labour, materials, energy and capital. As highlighted in Chapter Two, economic production has caused pollution and waste, degraded natural habitats and depleted natural resources to an extent that our future survival is now considered to be under threat.

In the formulation of environmental policies economic methods have been used to demonstrate the costs and benefits to society. This has required placing an economic value on nature. Ecological economics has emerged as a new sub-discipline to address the interdependence of economies and ecosystems. In particular, how these two systems co-evolve based on the principles of sustainable development (see Chapter One).

The use of land and natural resources was considered a key aspect of national wealth in classical economic theory which did not recognise the wider concept of the 'environment' as we understand it today. Political economist Adam Smith ([1776]1998) singled out rent from the use of land as a source of revenue 'more stable and permanent' than interest from money or profits from stock. As countries industrialised the focus of economic theory moved to wage labour and capital stock. Karl Marx described land as providing a reservoir of resources (for example, coal and minerals) which provided natural power to drive mills and was an element of production in agriculture (Harvey, 2006). Availability of land and, implicitly, food was a particular concern of early classical economists such as Anne-Robert-Jacques Turgot who outlined a law of diminishing returns in agriculture, arguing that there was a maximum point of land productivity that was impossible to surpass. This implied that the amount of available land placed a constraint on population and wealth, an idea argued by Thomas Malthus in *An essay on the principle of population as it affects the future improvement of society* (1798). Malthus believed society would be under permanent threat of starvation unless measures were taken to limit population expansion. He saw population growth, driven initially by surplus food production, eventually to be constrained by limits to productive land use resulting in food shortage.

As nations industrialised, economists became concerned about the limits to industrial and agricultural productivity. John Stuart Mill was among the first economists to treat the environment as more than a unit of land or a means of production. He championed the 'stationary state economy' and warned against the drive for unlimited economic growth. Later, economist Arthur C Pigou (1932) argued that when the detrimental effects of an activity went unrecognised then the government should intervene. He described these detrimental effects as 'negative externalities' and in doing so introduced a concept that is now central to modern ecological economics (Pearce and Turner, 1990).

In his essay 'The economics of the coming spaceship Earth' (1966) KE Boulding challenged neoclassical economic ideas of an 'open' economic system without finite resources and a limited assimiliative capacity to absorb waste (O'Riordan and Turner, 1983). He called the open economy a 'cowboy' economy, symboblic of a cowboy's 'reckless, exploitatvive, romantic and violent behaviour'. He saw the closed economy of the future as a 'spaceman' economy where the Earth is a single spaceship with limited reservoirs of resources and capacity to deal with pollution (Deese, 2009).

Boulding's use of the spaceship Earth metaphor made the resource limitations of the economic system understandable to a wider public. At the same time, the mathematical economist Nicholas Georgescu-Roegen applied similar ideas to economic theory. In *The entropy law and the economic process* (1971), Georgescu-Roegen explained that whenever energy is used, the amount of usable energy available to society declines. This argument is based on the second law of thermodynamics which states that although energy cannot be created or destroyed, it can be dispersed in less usable forms. Industrial activity disperses energy by transforming available but limited energy sources (such as fossil fuels) into waste. Accordingly, the amount of easily available fuel is continuously dwindling away; eventually the limited stock of fossil fuels on which modern society is dependant will have to be substituted by other renewable sources of energy such as solar power. Georgescu-Roegen developed a bioeconomic programme which emphasised the importance of viable technologies that could maintain economic activity over the long term without using non-renewable resources (Gowdy and Mesner, 1998). This argument was shared by EF Schumacher, who championed the use of appropriate technology in *Small is beautiful: A study of economics as if people mattered* (1973). Like Georgescu-Roegen, Schumacher argued that natural resources should be treated as capital not expandable income. By utilising resources on an industrial scale, and at an unprecedented speed, society was mining its natural capital rather than living off its dividend. What was needed instead was an ecologically efficient distribution of resources that maximised human wellbeing over time with the aim to obtain the maximum amount of wellbeing with the minimum amount of consumption.

Pricing nature

Economists have sought to reflect the value of the environment to society by attributing a monetary value to ecosystem services. It has been used to demonstrate the marginal social costs and benefits of policies and programmes. Cost–benefit analysis has been widely used by government agencies responsible for environmental regulations to make the case for environmental protection. However, its application can be complex and controversial and is not always trusted by environmental campaigners or regulated industries (Hanley and Barbier, 2009).

In 1970 MIT's *Study of critical environmental problems* (SCEP, 1970) used a structured approach to communicate the multiple values of the environment. It described nine 'environmental services' that would decline if the functioning of ecosystems were damaged. These ideas were developed and applied to biodiversity assessments and used as a core concept of the Millennium Ecosystem Assessment (MEA) (2005). The MEA examined the consequences of ecosystem change on human wellbeing, and provided a global overview of conditions of the world's ecosystems and the services they provide for humanity. It defined the four categories of ecosystem services that contribute to human wellbeing as: (1) provisioning services, such as food; (2) regulating services, such as filtration of pollutants and flood control; (3) cultural services, such as recreation; and (4) supporting services, such as soil formation and photosynthesis.

The ecosystem services approach has enabled ecological functions such as pollination and climate regulation to be translated into economic terms determining their human utility and value. It restates the economic significance of the environment as a provider of the basic material for human wellbeing, supporting health and social relations, providing security, and creating the conditions for freedom of choice and action. However, it does not overcome the problem of setting a market price that reflects services that are not traded in the market. An attempt has been made to estimate the value of ecosystem services provided by Earth's biosphere. Ecosystem services have been estimated to be worth US$16–54 trillion/year to humanity. The majority of these services are still outside the market economy (Costanza et al, 1987).

A key challenge for contemporary ecological economists is to ensure the value of the environment is captured through market signals that tax environmental 'bads' and support environmental 'goods'. Due to many ecosystem services not being recognised in the market system, the full cost of their degradation is not considered. Following Pigou, these negative externalities have been regarded as market failures and corrected. This is an argument that has been applied to a wide range of environmental policies from waste management to climate change. The 2006 Stern Review of the economics of climate change presented the economic case for environmental action (see Box 3.1).

Box 3.1: Economics of climate change

Climate change has been seen as has been the greatest market failure the world has ever seen (Stern, 2006). Stern's review of the economics of climate change estimated that the overall cost of not taking action would be equivalent to losing at least 5 per cent of global gross domestic product (GDP) each year, now and forever. When a wider range of risks and impacts are considered the *Review* stated that costs could rise to 20 per cent of GDP or more. In contrast the costs of preventative action, such as reducing greenhouse gas emissions could be limited to approximately 1 per cent of global GDP each year.

The discount rate used by Stern to value the future has been criticised. Discount rate allows the value of future costs and benefits in today's terms to be measured. A high discount rate indicates a preference for consumption now rather than in the future. The choice of an appropriate discount rate is key to assessing the extent of sacrifices the world should be taking now to prevent or slow down climate change damage affecting future generations (HCTC, 2008). Low discount rates make the future more important, high discount rates make it less so (Ackerman, 2009). Stern used a near zero discount rate to underpin his argument, this was an ethically driven decision that reflected the long term impact of climate change on future generations. Other economists used much higher discount rates that led them to conclude that Stern's approach was inefficient because early action is more expensive than necessary (Nordhaus, 2008). The varying conclusions that the application of different discount rates can bring mean that it is the discount rate which is the most important single number in climate economics (Ackerman, 2009). As an alternative approach, some economists argue that climate change policy should be treated as an insurance against worst case scenarios rather than a measure that can be subjected to cost–benefit analysis.

No growth economics

The relentless pursuit of economic growth has been seen as endangering the long-term survival of the human species (Jackson, 2009). Alternative systems have been put forward where policies are designed explicitly to achieve social and environmental goals and where growth is a by-product (NEF, 2006). Daly (2008) presented an alternative approach to the conventional growth paradigm in the form of the steady-state economy (SSE) (see Box 3.2). He argued traditional growth has expanded the economy to a size that must now conform to global environmental constraints. Further economic growth will be uneconomic because it will produce more social and environmental costs than it does benefits. A SSE is seen as a system that supports qualitative development but not quantitative growth; it produces better outcomes not more outputs. This shift in focus has had little impact on the way policy makers think about measuring progress in society.

Box 3.2: The steady-state economy

An SSE is an economy with constant population and constant stock of capital, maintained by a low rate of throughput that is within the regenerative and assimilative capacities of the ecosystem (Daly, 2008).

Attempts have been made at 'decoupling', or breaking the link between economic growth and worsening environmental quality (NEF, 2006; OECD, 2002). Theoretically this could be achieved by reconfiguring production processes and redesigning goods and services. In doing so, it is hoped that the economy can continue to grow without exceeding ecological limits. Decoupling may lead to increased resource efficiency, use of renewable energy and reduction in material output. However, critics have argued that decoupling has become the acceptable face of sustainability and that it is a myth to suggest that growth can continue without the need for a fundamental restructuring of economic and social systems.

In *Prosperity without growth* Jackson (2009) argues that a different kind of economy is essential for a different kind of prosperity – one where human beings can flourish within the ecological limits of a finite planet. He argues that the growth economy is driven by the consumption and production of novelty which locks society into an iron cage of consumerism. Change at the personal and societal level is necessary to make the transition to a new form of prosperity that does not depend on unrelenting growth. The structure of the market economy needs to be confronted if real environmental gains are to be achieved. There is a need for a fundamental change to the structure of society – a change on the scale achieved in the industrial revolution but driven by clean, efficient and sustainable renewable energy technologies. This will require establishing the ecological boundaries for human activity, abandoning growth economics and transforming the mass consumer culture.

Sociological perspectives

Sociological understandings of human interaction with our social, economic and natural environment are helpful in addressing contemporary environmental issues and policy development. Macnaghten and Urry (1995, 210) suggest

> in contrast to a naive realist perspective which assumes that environmental issues progressively come to light simply through the extension of scientific understandings, a sociologically informed inquiry looks to the cultural and

political conditions out of which environmental issues emerge, and thereby to a more informed account of the social consequences.

In the early 1990s environmental sociology developed as a 'sub discipline' of sociology to study the social factors that cause environmental problems, the societal impacts of those problems, and efforts to find solutions. Particular attention has been given to the social processes by which certain environmental conditions become socially defined as problems. These include examining the role of science, technology and institutions as well as institutional practices (see, for example, Redclift and Benton, 1994; or Irwin, 2001). Sociologists often begin with basic questions that are normally taken for granted such as 'What is the environment?' and whether it can be considered as an objective entity that is separate from the social (Dunlap, 2010, 16). The following section will provide a brief introduction to core debates covered in sociology. These are: understanding the human–environment relationship, the relationship between science, technology, risk and sociology; and how sociology can inform environmental policy decisions.

The human–environment relationship

Classical social theory generally has a problematic relationship with the environment. The notable theories that can be related to the environment come from the 'usual triumvirate of Marx, Weber and Durkheim' (Irwin, 2001, 5). One of the main aspects of social theory's problematic relationship with the environment is that as Redclift and Woodgate (1994, 53) suggest 'for the founding fathers' of modern sociology the natural environment, was, on the whole, defined negatively as 'that which was not social' and as a result was largely ignored within the discipline.

However, numerous sociologists make reference to the influential 1991 lecture by Howard Newby (the then head of the UK Economics and Social Research Council), 'One world, two cultures', where he challenged the British Sociological Association to engage in environmental thinking (see Benton and Redcliffe, 1994; Irwin, 2001;

Shove, 2010). To many, this inspired changes within the field. Indeed, in the 1990s, two key shifts took place where structuralists began to consider how people were a 'product' of their environment, and those within the interpretist tradition began to challenge the view that the environment was a physical entity that could not be altered by humans (Redclift and Woodgate, 1994, 53–4). Further, the application of Anthony Giddens' structuration framework to the human–environment relationship enabled the environment to be viewed as a structure that humans operate within, but also one in which human agency may lead to environmental change (Redclift and Woodgate, 1994, 53–4).

The way in which the environment is conceptualised underpins how we address scientific understanding of environmental change, human impacts and policy responses (Dunlap, 2010, 23). Sociologists who consider the 'sociocultural' constructions of the environment focus on underlying values and beliefs rather than actual conditions. These sociologists take an 'agnostic' approach to the existence (or not) of environmental problems compared to 'environmental pragmatists' who focus on the science–policy relationships, dynamics and deconstruction of scientific claims (Dunlap, 2010, 23). The realism versus constructivism debate was significant in the environmental sociology field in the 1990s. This debate became heated where constructivists were 'depicted as a sort of Darth Vader, perverting the force of sociological understanding and ignoring the "reality" of the environmental crisis' (Hannigan, 2006, 29). Such a debate 'led to silly and sterile arguments about whether there is or is not a real world and whether scientific knowledge bears any relation to it (if it exists)' (Oreskes, 2004, 1241). However, it has been argued that constructivists were misunderstood as much of their argument was that 'bestowing absolute certainty solely on the basis of a scientific head count is perilous' (Hannigan, 2006, 30). Since the 1990s critical realists have accepted that *understandings* of environmental problems are socially constructed, but that science is able to provide important evidence about real world conditions (Dunlap, 2010, 20).

While these debates may appear academic, they do have an important application to policy. For example, McLaughlin and Dietz (2008, 102) apply constructivist perspectives when considering vulnerability to environmental hazards: 'the constructivist perspective on vulnerability emphasizes the role that culture plays in shaping definitions of and exposure to risk'. They argue that a purely 'realist' approach to risk assumes that risk is an objective phenomenon, whereas the constructivist perspective considers the interactions between certain (also socially constructed) categories such as class, gender and race.

Science, technology and sociology

As described above, constructivists have been criticised for their 'agnostic' stance on the validity of 'factual' information. However, they have much to offer when it comes to understanding the development and dissemination of scientific evidence, and its translation into policy. Those who study the sociology of scientific knowledge (SSK) argue that 'the 'facts' of environmental matters do not speak for themselves: instead they are actively created and interpreted' (Irwin, 2001, 74). Within the SSK literature considerations are given to various processes and relationships (see Irwin, 2001; Hannigan, 2006; or Wynne, 1994) including:

- the social and organisational context within which scientists operate – for example, their academic discipline, their location (industry, academia and policy);
- the political and economic context within which scientists operate – for example, funding sources and political priorities;
- the nature of the 'epistemic' community – the dominance of particular models, schools of thought and interests.

A range of factors therefore shape, reshape and reform 'facts'. For example, a scientist working within industry will be influenced by the priorities of that industry (for example, profit, rapid innovation and so on) and will be unlikely to champion research findings that have a negative impact on these priorities (Hannigan, 2006). While academic scientists may be unconstrained by such factors they are also products of their environment. The discipline that they work in (for example, geography, meteorology, biology, ecological economics and ecology) is likely to influence and shape research priorities, methodologies and assumptions about existing knowledge in the field. Equally, sources of available funding will also influence the types of research that are conducted. In an increasingly competitive economic environment, academic scientists may be driven by prescriptions and priorities laid down by funding bodies. Equally, where receiving non-public funds (for example, from charities or the private sector), academic scientists may be faced with very narrow project aims and funder assumptions or presumptions about what they should find.

There are also questions about the nature of the 'epistemic community' (that is, knowledge community), how it is made up, what interests it underrepresents (or indeed deliberately excludes), and how this is reflected in policy developments. For example, Hannigan (2006) identifies how assessment panels such as the IPCC do not always reflect the makeup of the research community or the full range of claims made by this community, and favours particular types of climate models 'found in a handful of large research laboratories often associated with meteorological offices' (Hannigan, 2006, 102–3). Given these issues, Wynne asks the question 'do the epistemical commitments on which the scientific knowledge is built serve to constrain the vision of what is at stake?' (1994, 172).

There are also questions about *who* should/or is able to contribute to knowledge, for example, Irwin (2001, 72) suggests that 'science is used to stifle other voices within environmental discussion'. However, there has been a significant shift in policy towards science communication, public engagement, and citizen science where the public is no longer regarded as a passive receptor of environmental policy (or indeed environmental problems). Agenda 21, one of the principle outputs of the 1992 Rio Earth Summit, highlighted the importance of public engagement with both the identification of problems, and policy development (see Chapter Four). Indeed, it is argued that 'lay' knowledge (that is, the knowledge of those exposed to particular circumstances on a regular basis) can improve policy outcomes. Wynne's influential study of the impact of Chernobyl nuclear fallout on the sheep farming industry in Cumbria (UK) found that laboratory testing had not considered the specifics of hill farming in this area, and that scientists 'made unqualified reassuring assertions that had then been proven mistaken' (1996, 26). Simple factual information such as how sheep move between fields, where they are kept, whether they are constrained to certain areas was not gathered. Wynne (1996, 35) argued that better decisions could have been made if 'only the experts could have recognised and accepted lay expertise (in this case, speaking to the farmers about the "on the ground" experiences). Instead, lay knowledge was downgraded and the local experts with their situational specific knowledge were sidelined.'

Sociology and environmental policy

So far we have discussed some of the ways in which sociological understandings can inform environmental policy (and explain to some extent policy trajectories), however, there is also a growing literature base that is directly related to policy. First, as described above, there is a distinct literature that focuses on the importance of 'lay' knowledge. This literature runs alongside a more general shift within the international policy community (and often national, federal, regional and local) towards a greater inclusion of non-experts within decision-making processes. Second, sociologists consider how, at the institutional level, *thinking* about the environment varies across time and space. As Redclift and Woodgate suggest, 'the discourse surrounding the environment and development…reflect[s] both divergent historical experiences and different interpretation of those experiences. In the North, countries have adopted their own language to describe problems in the South' (1994, 64).

Third, and closely related, at the national level sociology can help us to understand 'the social processes which currently produce what we recognise as environmental damage' (Macnaghten and Urry, 1995, 212), for example, helping us to understand consumption patterns, market flows and social norms. As Spaargaren (2003, 687) puts it, there has been a trend 'to attach greater importance to the role of citizen-consumers in shaping and reproducing some of the core institutions of production and consumption', and through this, a growth in the literature base that deconstructs environmental attitudes and behaviours. In the UK, this academic literature base runs parallel to (and critiques) policy attempts to understand and influence environmental behaviours. In the 1990s and 2000s policy tended to focus on a linear 'ABC' (attitude → behaviour → choice) model of behavioural change, assuming 'information deficit' as the main problem, and that by informing, and influencing attitudes, behavioural changes and greener choices would be made. However, influential sociologists such as Shove (2010) argue that this understanding is flawed, and that environmental attitudes and behaviours operate in a far more complex environment than suggested by the ABC model. Instead, Shove argues, it is essential that attention is given to understanding how consumer needs and aspirations develop over time, how systems of provision such as food, water and energy shape and restrict behaviours, and how and when radical changes (in policy, availability of resources and so on) have occurred in the past and have influenced behaviour (2010, 5–6). In sum, Shove suggests that 'co-evolutionary accounts of change do not deny the possibility of meaningful policy action, but at a minimum they recognise that effect is never in isolation and that interventions go on within, not outside, the processes they seek to shape' (2010: 6). Box 3.3 describes this type of approach and its possible applications in more detail.

Box 3.3: Using social practice theory to explore sustainable lifestyles

Social practice theory suggests that we pay attention to norms, habits, social networks, infrastructures and the wider social, technical and economic systems that influence our lifestyles and cause them to change over time. These ideas were explored in a project called 'Careers of action on climate change' which examined why individuals adopt low-carbon lifestyles, and how these develop throughout their lives. The study investigated why such changes occurred, and found that past experience played a key role in shaping present lifestyles, partly through 'learning-by-doing'. For example, some people were taught to 'make-do-and mend' as children and continued to develop these practical skills throughout their lives. The study used Bourdieu's (1984) concept of 'habitus', a set of dispositions acquired through practice, to explore these processes. It found that three forms of habitus, called the 'simplicity', 'ecological' and 'radical' habitus, helped shape action on climate change.

A second theme concerned social interactions and the need to 'co-ordinate' practices with others. For example, a person's food choices may be affected by the people with whom they live. Furthermore, the study found an important role played by 'communities of practice' (groups of people who perform an activity together) such as campaign organisations and green lifestyle groups. These were important sites for people to discuss ideas and practices, learn from others and perhaps be drawn into a trajectory of increasing commitment. Finally, careers of action on climate change were strongly shaped by their contexts, including opportunities and constraints provided by geographical surroundings (such as shops, cycle-paths, hills and even the weather). Historical context also played a part; for example, social discourses about climate change have evolved over time, as has technology. A related theme was biographical time; people's lifestyles were strongly shaped by their life-stage, and the roles, responsibilities and 'moments of change' that this entailed.

These findings suggest that rather than focusing solely on mass-scale information provision, policy measures should provide opportunities for hands-on learning and ensure that infrastructures are in place to facilitate sustainable lifestyles. Policy could also promote learning through social networks, as used by the charity Global Action Plan in their EcoTeams.
(Written by Sarah Royston (née Hards) and adapted from Hards, 2011; 2012)

Social policy perspectives

The relationship between the environment and economics is clearly established one, as are some of the more philosophical, normative questions raised by environmental sociologists. However, the link between social policy and environmental policy may be less apparent. Social policy has traditionally been seen as the 'handmaiden' to politics and economics (Fitzpatrick, 2011, 3). In addition, the social policy–environmental policy relationship is not helped by the broad and interdisciplinary nature of both environmental studies and social policy with issues often appearing within or at the fringes of the fields of geography, development, planning, health, politics or sociology.

However, social policy is central to the study of environmental policy, as without the help of social policy perspectives, environmental policies run the risk of being regressive, unpalatable and, ultimately, failing. As Fitzpatrick and Cahill (2002, 13) argue, while social policy makers have previously pursued policies at the cost of the environment, if a similarly blinkered mentality is pursued by environmental policy makers then 'they may only be repeating the [same] underlying mistake'. In addition to the deliberate attempts to draw together social and environmental policy, there are also implicit synergies in the language of social policy and sustainable development. Huby (1998) identifies three key similarities, a focus on inequality, sustainability and responsibility. First, the distribution of resources is a key concern of social policy, and are also central to discussions about development and the environment since many argue that poverty can exacerbate pollution and degradation. Second, the concept of sustainable development chimes with both fields, as it concerns meeting needs, issues of fairness, risk and uncertainty. Third, debates of justice, individual and social responsibility are echoed within both fields (see also Cahill, 2002; Fitzpatrick and Cahill, 2002).

Four relationships between social policy and environmental policy can be outlined: first, how social policy can be helpful in the study of environmental policy; second, environmental dimensions of social change; third, social dimensions of environmental change; and fourth, the challenge of balancing social and environmental policies.

What is social policy and how does it relate to environmental policy?

Hudson et al (2008, ix) outlined how 'social policy is an interdisciplinary subject that draws on the knowledge base and concepts of the core social sciences with a focus on the analysis of social problems'. These social problems have traditionally divided into five welfare pillars: social security, employment, housing, education and health, and grounded in William Beveridge's five giants 'want, idleness, squalor, ignorance, and disease' that threatened UK wellbeing after the Second World War (Hudson et al, 2008, 7). However, since the 1990s social policy academics have challenged this relatively narrow focus, stressing the need to consider other issues such as the inter-relationship between society and the environment, and how changes to one can affect the other (Huby, 1998).

As discussed in Chapter Two, there is a clear relationship between the drivers of environmental change and social impacts, especially between social inequality, inequity and environmental damage. Social policy is considered ideally placed to compensate for unjust social problems due to its role in rectifying market-based failures and inequalities (Gough and Marden, 2011, 15). Fitzpatrick and Cahill (2002, 12) outlined a number of positive lessons that social policy can 'teach' environmentalism. First, social policy's pragmatic, applied nature considers the existing policy environment and how to improve on this, rather than providing 'utopian' policy solutions. Second, it deconstructs negative human impacts on the environment, considering the effects of inequality and socio-economic systems on the environment rather than simply regarding all humans as having an equally negative impact. Third, it makes certain presumptions about the necessary social outcomes of environmental policies, in that human need and society must be considered within environmental policy solutions: 'there is little point in preserving resources if the price is either scarcity for all or health and security for some' (Fitzpatrick and Cahill, 2002, 12).

Environmental dimensions of social change

Social policy arose as a response to industrialisation which witnessed large-scale changes in resource use, pollution and associated impacts on human health and wellbeing: 'social policy emerged in the nineteenth century as a response to the social problems produced by the impact of humanity on the environment' (Cahill, 2002, 3). Most industrialised countries have a pattern of deforestation, species loss, soil degradation, water and air pollution that mirrors periods and processes of industrialisation (Snell and Quinn, 2011, 292). Box 3.4 demonstrates the benefits brought by development and associated environmental and social impacts. Similar stories are evident in the impact of the transport sector on human health and wellbeing (for example, WHO, 2005), the impact of environmental pollution on food safety (for example, Makokha, 2008), and the effect of human development on climate change (for example, UNEP, 2010).

Box 3.4: Industrialisation, pollution and its effects

Merseyside, in the North West of England, provides an example of the relationship between societal change and environmental impacts. During the eighteenth century the geography of the area (a long, wide estuary) meant that it was ideally placed for imports and exports (for more detail see Hyde, 1971 or Langton, 1983), and development around the area increased substantially. Development continued through the nineteenth and twentieth centuries, and by the 1900s there was a booming chemical industry in the area. While industrialisation changed the natural environment through water pollution, loss of land for development, and air pollution, until the economic decline of the 1970s, industry provided secure jobs, and economic prosperity. However, since the decline of industry in the 1970s, focus has shifted from the benefits of the chemical industry to the negative effects of living in a polluted environment (for example see NWRA, 2004). Over the last 40 years there has been significant concern about the impact of pollution on both health, housing and security. While it is impossible to draw definitive links, Shaw et al (2008) found unusually high levels of respiratory problems and cancers which are typically associated with pollutants in the air, soil and water. In addition to this, the safety of chemical disposal measures has been brought into question with some areas facing evacuation and resettlement following the discovery of lethal gasses escaping from chemical dumps (see *Guardian*, 2000, for more information).

Developing and newly industrialised countries also face similar questions about how to balance environmental and economic concerns. In the 2012 International Energy Agency annual report, China's greenhouse gas emissions were found to have increased by 9.3 per cent, and India's by 8.7 per cent. Overall China, the US, the EU and India respectively were the largest four emitters globally (IEA, 2012b). Climate agreements at the global level are often dominated by discussions about the extent to which developing and newly industrialised countries should be 'allowed' to continue to develop, and the extent to which environmental degradation associated with development should be prevented (see Chapters Four and Five).

It is important to note that industrialisation occurs within a global context, and some argue that previous colonial relationships are played out in trade conflicts between developed and developing countries (Baker, 2006, 159), where trade restrictions, debt burdens, and a fall in commodity prices encourage the increased production of certain goods, resulting in rapid environmental degradation (Snell and Quinn, 2011, 296). It should also be noted that as many developed countries such as the UK have reduced their industrial sector, they have 'outsourced' production to newly industrialised economies, become more dependent on imports (Hermann and Hauschild, 2009). This is important as it demonstrates that developed countries are still contributing to environmental degradation through consumption, even if they no longer directly cause it on their territory (see Roberts and Parks, 2007, 177).

In Europe, urbanisation, 'the large shifts of people in rural to urban areas' is said to have started at the time of the industrial revolution (Gelderblom and Kok, 1994, 139). Gelderblom and Kok (1994) discuss the impact of rapid urbanisation in South Africa in the 1990s, outlining the social effects of overcrowding, insufficient services, and poor environmental quality in urban areas as the population begins to outstrip the space and resources available. In developing and newly industrialised countries these processes are occurring more quickly. In addition to overcrowded, polluted and unprepared social and physical infrastructures within cities (see Chapter Two), urbanisation has severe implications for those living in rural areas, both in terms of population loss, and also changes in land use as previously rural areas are given over to development. China is an example of a country undergoing rapid urbanisation and has witnessed significant amounts of rural land converted to urban development (Tang et al, 2008). Not only do industrialisation and urbanisation have immediate social impacts such as the reduction of food production and greater dependence on imports, it also clearly has a negative impact on the environment (see Hubacek et al, 2009).

Environmental justice

The social dimensions of environmental change are also a central aspect of the social–environmental policy relationship. Huby (1998, 3) suggests social policy's focus on the 'fault lines' of society, structured inequalities, can help in understanding how the consequences of environmental problems are felt by different sections of society. In the 1980s the environmental justice movement developed in the US, where links began to be made between occurrences of pollution and racial background (Agyeman, 2002, 35). Bullard (1999, 6) outlined environmental racism as 'any environmental policy, practice, or directive that differentially affects or disadvantages (whether intended or unintended) individuals, groups or communities based on race or colour'. The term environmental (in)justice has spread to the UK and other developed countries. In addition to race and ethnicity the term has been extended to poverty, inequality and age issues.

The UK Friends of the Earth (FoE) 1999 study on environmental pollution acted as a launch pad for the UK environmental justice movement. FoE mapped the number of 'polluting' factories (defined as those registered under the Integrated Pollution Control (IPC) framework) against income data (see Figure 3.1). High levels of carcinogens were found to be emitted in the most deprived 10 per cent of UK local authorities, suggesting that those exposed most to the negative effects of pollution were the poorest (Bullock et al 2000). In fact, the poorest families are twice as likely to have a polluting factory close by than those with average household incomes over £60,000 (Bullock et al, 2000, 1).

There have been substantial developments in the environmental justice movement which have included a range of social (that is, race, ethnicity, class, income, social housing, older people, children and indigenous peoples) and environmental dimensions (that is, air pollution, landfill sites, incinerators, contaminated land and flooding) (Walker, 2012, 2).

Figure 3.1: Pollution and postcodes

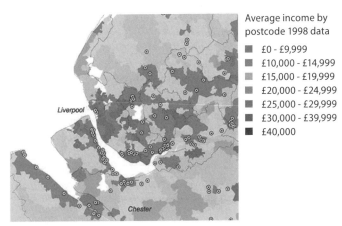

Source: Friends of the Earth, 1999

Research on flooding found that those people living on tidal floodplains in England are eight times more likely to be in the most deprived areas despite these groups often being least able to prepare for such events, or to recover from them (for example, in terms of accessing/purchasing house insurance) (Walker et al, 2003). Transport and environment research has shown that the wealthiest groups are most likely to have access to a car. The burden of vehicle pollution falls on the poorest groups, who do not have access to a car, but are exposed to air pollutants and suffer associated health effects, and are likely to be killed or seriously injured on the road (Huby, 1998; Jephcote and Chen, 2011; White et al, 2000).

There are a number of explanations as to why environmental injustices occur. Walker (2012, 64) summarises these as contextual process claims and structural process claims. Contextual claims consider how a particular form of pollution (and exposure to it) has occurred. For example, in Merseyside (UK) the geography of the area lent itself to occupying a key role during the industrial revolution, both as a gateway for imports and exports, and in the last century as an area ideal for particular chemical processes. It is also likely that as with many industrial areas, low cost housing was built close to these areas for those working in the factories, and that these are now one of the cheapest forms of housing.

Structural process claims consider whether structural inequalities in society have led to environmental inequalities. Again, using the Merseyside example, it is likely that the location of low-cost housing in poor areas, and the financial mobility of higher income groups will mean that such areas are those which are least desirable (see NWDA, 2004). While neither claim fully explains environmental injustices, together, both provide some degree of insight. There are also challenges for policy makers that emerge from the environmental justice debate. First, the question of how environmental goods and bads *should* be distributed, and second the question of who should, and who actually does decide on their distribution (Walker, 2012, 42–4).

Balancing social and environmental policies

Given the proportion of public spending on welfare, arguably, social policies themselves should be delivered in a more environmentally sustainable manner (and in recent years, the move towards ecological modernisation may have supported this). Indeed, a number of green critiques of social policy focus on growth, employment and centralisation (see Fitzpatrick and Cahill, 2002, 12; Fitzpatrick, 2011). It is undeniable that social policies have an environmental impact, as Cahill suggests 'Social Policy is concerned with the satisfaction of human needs...the meeting of need has an environmental impact' (2002, 2). Indeed, a number of social policy academics raise the importance of greening welfare services themselves (see Gough and Meadowcroft, 2011; Fitzpatrick, 2011 for a discussion of the carbon emissions of the British National Health Service).

While social policies may contribute towards environmental problems, they can also be used to redress/adjust for some of the inequalities associated with the effects of pollution (as identified above). The balancing of social and environmental policy objectives is a significant challenge. The reconciliation of fuel poverty and climate change objectives in the UK is an example of this challenge (see Box 3.5). If handled alone, fuel poverty policy can have a negative impact on the environment, and climate policy can have a negative impact on the poorest in society. However, dealing with the two policy objectives simultaneously, policy outcomes can be better balanced. While in reality there are numerous challenges associated with this balancing act, and policy interventions are rarely perfectly targeted or effective, the case study demonstrates the possibility of bringing together two policy areas that would have been dealt with in isolation in the past.

Box 3.5: Balancing UK fuel poverty and climate change commitments

In the UK, fuel poverty is defined as being present in a 'household that has to spend more than 10 per cent of its income on all fuel to keep warm' (DTI, 2001, 6). Britain has the highest number of avoidable deaths due to winter cold in Western Europe, and the UK has a legally binding commitment to eliminate fuel poverty by 2016. In addition, the Climate Change Act (2008) means that the UK has a legally binding duty to reduce greenhouse gas emissions by 80 per cent by 2050. There are two main approaches that can be applied to address fuel poverty; reduce the costs of energy bills (through subsidisation, benefits or discounts), or reduce the necessity to use as much energy (through energy efficiency measures). Equally, the central policy outcome that climate change legislation requires is a reduction of energy use. However, there is potential conflict between fuel poverty alleviation and climate change mitigation. Where fuel poverty is dealt with in isolation it may lead to increased carbon emissions. For example, subsidising energy bills may result in warmer homes and the mitigation of fuel poverty, but this may also lead to overall increases in energy use. Equally, climate change mitigation policies that do not consider the needs of the fuel poor may have a disproportionate affect them (Snell and Thomson, 2013, 24). It is broadly recognised that the most effective solutions to both policy issues are those that recognise their interaction (for example, Huby, 1998; Cahill, 2002; Fitzpatrick, 2011; Snell and Thomson, 2013). In order to meet both policy objectives simultaneously, government has focused on policies that support energy efficiency measures, providing free or highly subsidised measures to the poorest households that cannot afford such home improvements. While policy in this area is not without criticism, addressing both goals simultaneously reduces regressive environmental policies and the negative impact of social policies (see Snell and Thomson, 2013).

In the last decade social policy academics have begun to discuss the idea of 'eco-social policy'. While this is a very small literature base which typically spills into other disciplines it provides ideas about radically balancing social and environmental policies. It also furthers the idea of ecological modernisation and policy integration (see Chapter One). It is argued that there has been progress towards environmental policy making, and that while an 'eco-state' has emerged (for example, a recognition at the policy level of the importance of environmental policies) this has been superficially imposed on existing policy making processes which are typically fragmented and disjointed (Gough et al, 2008). Equally, while some states have made progress at integrating environmental concerns into broader public/social policy thinking, this has usually been among the social democratic welfare states such as Denmark and the Netherlands rather than liberal market economies with less comprehensive social provision (Gough et al, 2008, 330). Similar shifts in policy will be more challenging for countries with market-based economies such as the UK (Gough, 2011, 62).

Beyond ecological modernisation or policy integration, more radical arguments about the decommodification of capitalism are made (that is, reducing dependence on the market through labour). Gough and Meadowcroft suggest that a second phase of decommodification (the first occurring through the creation of welfare states) could, in the case of the need to reduce carbon emissions, enable 'a move towards de-commodified *production* – reducing working hours and commodity purchases, developing "co-production"' (2011). Also, as outlined by the New Economics Foundation (NEF), there is the potential for a 'Green New Deal' in the light of the economic downturn, bringing together state, market, ecosystems and civil society. In reality, radical ideas such as those proposed by the NEF (2008, 81), which advocates major investment in housing stock, creation of 'green collar jobs' and the re-pricing of carbon to reflect true costs, are unlikely to be implemented in the short term as they reflect such a significant shift from existing societal structures, political and social norms (Fitzpatrick and Cahill 2002). However, such thinking represents a worthy 'thought experiment' (Fitzpatrick, 2002, 81; see also Fitzpatrick and Cahill, 2002).

SUMMARY

■ Capitalism and the quest for economic growth have been criticised for failing to reconcile the objectives of human development, poverty reduction and environmental sustainability.

■ Economists have sought to reflect the value of the environment to society by attributing a monetary value to ecosystem services.

■ Alternative systems have been put forward where policies are designed explicitly to achieve social and environmental goals and where growth is a by-product.

■ Sociology provides us with numerous theoretical approaches that can help to understand the relationship between society, the environment, science and policy.

■ Theories of constructivism have been used by sociologists to demonstrate how scientific evidence is not generated in a vacuum, but is influenced by a range of social, economic and political factors.

■ Sociologists argue that environmentally damaging behaviours are not simply the result of a lack of knowledge about greener alternatives.

■ Social policy understandings can be helpful in the study of environmental policy, particularly in terms of stressing the importance of understanding current social and policy circumstances, and how to improve on these.

■ Social policy also draws attention to the differential impacts of environmental change.

■ The effects of social change on the environment can also be considered through a social policy lens, considering the impact of industrialisation and urbanisation on the environment and on human welfare.

■ Social policy draws attention to the environmental impact of public spending and how to reconcile potentially competing policy needs.

READING GUIDE

Cahill, M, 2002, The environment and social policy, London: Routledge

Fitzpatrick, T (ed), 2011, *Understanding the environment and social policy*, Bristol: Policy Press

Fitzpatrick, T, Cahill, M (eds), 2002, *Environment and welfare*, Basingstoke: Palgrave Macmillan

Huby, M, 1998, *Social policy and the environment*, Oxford: Oxford University Press

Pigou, AC, 2006, *The economics of welfare: Volume I*, New York: Cosimo Classics

Redclift, M, Benton, T (eds), 1994, *Social theory and the global environment*, London: Routledge

Redclift, M, Woodgate, G, 2010, *The international handbook of environmental sociology*, 2nd edn, Cheltenham: Edward Elgar

SCEP (Study of Critical Environmental Problems), 1970, Man's impact on the global environment, Study of Critical Environmental Problems, Cambridge, MA: MIT Press

Scott, J, Marshall, G, 2009, Oxford dictionary of sociology, Oxford: Oxford University Press

Sutton, PW, 2007, *The environment: A sociological introduction*, Cambridge: Polity Press

4

Making environmental policies

Introduction

The tools, mechanisms and instruments available to policy makers vary significantly according to the scale of the problem. Where international action is necessary nation states have to agree that there is enough of a problem to justify action before beginning a long process of agreeing how to act. Decision-making is often complex, contentious, slow moving, and usually takes place through the emergence of 'international regimes'. National and local level policy is also fraught with difficulties, however it is generally characterised by the use of a particular set of policy instruments (expenditure, regulation, market-based tools, and voluntary agreements). This chapter considers international policy responses using the example of climate change policy, briefly outlines the role of supranational bodies such as the EU, and then discusses the use of different policy instruments at the national level.

Environmental policies: international responses

Given the increased awareness of environmental problems at the global level, cooperation between countries has become recognised as an essential part of environmental policy, and is reflected in many conferences, treaties and protocols (see Table 1.1). Lidskog and Sundquvist (2002, 79) found that there were 170 negotiated conventions covering a range of issues including: fisheries, ozone depletion, long-range air pollution, whaling and climate change. There are a number of stages and types of agreement that are typically discussed within the international environmental policy, these include:

■ Convention/treaty: contains binding obligations, rules and regulations;
■ Framework convention: usually contains a broad set of principles which is later developed further;
■ Protocol: spells out the specifics, for example, emission reduction targets (Carter, 2007, 245).

Barrett (1998) describes the steps involved in making international agreements as:

■ Pre-negotiation: manoeuvring and positioning by states, where viewpoints are often set out;
■ Negotiation: where conventions and protocols are discussed and agreed, often by more than 150 states;
■ Ratification: which usually involves a state's parliamentary approval, and agreements are usually not legally binding without this;
■ Implementation: where legislation typically passes through domestic parliaments in order to meet commitments; and
■ Renegotiation: where unforeseen events arise that make targets/actions impossible, or where new scientific evidence may provide improved understandings about the problem and required forms of action.

International regimes

Given the lack of 'world government', international regimes are considered the most developed way for nation-states to respond to transboundary environmental problems (Lidskog and Sundquvist, 2002, 79) and constitute 'a system of principles, norms, rules, operating procedures, and institutions that actors create or accept to regulate and coordinate action in a particular issue area of international relations' (Downie, 2011, 70). These elements are developed, organised and implemented through a number of different mechanisms and processes ranging from formal agreements, the creation of international organisations and accepted norms. Regimes can be identified in a range of environmental areas, and have a wide number of associated actors, institutions and procedures. Global climate policy is an example of an international environmental regime:

> The climate change regime seeks to mitigate human-induced climate change...Components of the climate regime include the principles, norms, rules, and procedures contained in the 1992 UN Framework Convention on Climate Change and the 1997 Kyoto Protocol as well as the international organizations interconnected with these agreements. (Downie, 2011, 74)

There are three key types of organisation/institution that are typically involved in international regime development: international organisations, non-governmental organisations (NGOs) and multinational companies, and governmental institutions (see Table 4.1).

Formal international environmental action is largely driven by the United Nations and its agencies (WRI, 2002, 138). UNEP has an overarching environmental mandate with the function of promoting 'cooperation on environmental policy between governments, UN agencies, other intergovernmental bodies and major groups and stakeholders' (UNEP, 2012). Typically, the bodies working under the umbrella of the UN build scientific consensus and set the agenda for negotiations, for example, the Intergovernmental Panel on Climate Change (IPCC) describes itself in the following terms:

> the leading international body for the assessment of climate change... [it] embodies a unique opportunity to provide rigorous and balanced scientific information to decision makers. By endorsing the IPCC reports, governments acknowledge the authority of their scientific content. The work of the organization is therefore policy-relevant and yet policy-neutral, never policy-prescriptive. (IPCC, 2012a)

The role of the nation state varies depending on both the environmental issue in question and the state itself. Where states have a clear interest in preventing an environmental problem from becoming worse they

Table 4.1: Typical organisations/institutions involved in international regime development

UN affiliated	United Nations Environment Programme (UNEP)
	United Nations Development Programme (UNDP)
	Commission on Sustainable Development (CSD)
	Food and Agriculture Organization (FAO)
	United Nations Educational, Scientific, and Cultural Organization (UNESCO)
	International Atomic Energy Agency (IAEA)
	Intergovernmental Panel on climate change (IPCC)
	World Health Organisation
Non governmental	World bank
	Regional Development Banks
	World Trade Organisation
	Global Environmental Facility
	International NGOs such as World Conservation Union
Governmental	Supranational organisations (for example, EU) and nation states

Source: Adapted from the World Resources Institute, 2002

may be a 'lead' state by promoting action at the international level. Typically, lead states are economically influential, and may also be driven by domestic politics to pursue stronger environmental policies. Lead states may also be what Castells and Ravetz refer to as *first-comer countries* (2001, 406). First-comer countries are those who are first to feel the effects of a transboundary environmental problem and so lead the international policy process in order to deal with the problem. However, the role the state plays varies significantly by issue (Carter, 2007, 256). Countries may also become 'veto' states that attempt to protect against any negative effects of environmental policies (and as a result, stall agreements) (see Carter, 2007, 256–7). Veto states may have particular interests that would be damaged if strict policies were introduced, for example, Japan is one of very few countries that continues to oppose the ban on commercial whaling on the grounds of both cultural, economic and scientific interests (see Danaher, 2002).

Non-state organisations (that is, the for-profit and not-for-profit sectors) also play a significant role at the international level. Both multinational company interests and NGO campaigns have attempted to feed into decision-making processes. Business interests are said to have both furthered and hindered international agreements, for example, Carter (2007, 257) suggests that the USA was encouraged during ozone negotiations by a major chemical manufacturer that saw financial opportunities if ozone depleting substances were banned. Equally, the role of environmental NGOs such as Sea Sheppard or Greenpeace during discussions about an international commercial whaling ban has been well documented (see Liddick, 2006, 17).

In some instances, the non-state sector may lead international environmental change, for example, through non-state certification programmes such as Forestry Stewardship Council (FSC) and Fair Trade certification. While these are voluntary schemes, companies may engage in these for a number of reasons including a reaction to NGO campaigning or environmental activism or an attempt to benefit from 'green' credentials or to pre-empt more stringent environmental standards (Gulbrandsen, 2010).

The following case study of climate negotiations considers the different elements that make up international agreements. Climate change agreements are generally high profile, controversial and have tended to receive significant media attention.

CASE STUDY FOUR

The UNFCCC (adopted in 1992)

The key international framework that addresses climate change is the United Nations Framework Convention on Climate Change (UNFCCC). The UNFCCC was in part developed as a response to the IPCC's first report in 1990, which called for a global treaty on climate change (UNFCCC, 2012a). Negotiations began shortly afterwards and in 1991 the intergovernmental negotiating committee (INC) met for the first time. At the 1992 Rio Earth Summit, the text of the UNFCCC was adopted, and opened for signatories. It came into force in 1994 and since then 195 countries have ratified it ('parties to the convention') (UNFCCC, 2012a). The key objective of the Convention is to stabilize greenhouse gas concentrations 'at a level that would prevent dangerous anthropogenic (human induced) interference with the climate system'. It states that 'such a level should be achieved within a time-frame sufficient to allow ecosystems to adapt naturally to climate change, to ensure that food production is not threatened, and to enable economic development to proceed in a sustainable manner' (UNFCCC, 2012b).

Box 4.1 presents some of the key aspects of the climate change convention.

Box 4.1: Key aspects of the United Nations Framework Convention on Climate Change (UNFCCC)

The UNFCCCC:

- recognises that there is a problem
- sets a lofty but specific goal
- puts the onus on developed countries to lead the way
- directs new funds to climate change activities in developing countries
- keeps tabs on the problem and what's being done about it
- charts the beginnings of a path to strike a delicate balance
- kicks off formal consideration of adaptation to climate change.

Source: adapted from UNFCCC, 2012b

The Convention distinguished between Annex I, non-Annex I, and Annex II countries. Annex I countries are largely developed nations. Annex I countries that belong to the OECD are also placed into Annex II. Annex II countries have the greatest commitment to act given both their historical contribution to the problem and their adoption of the non-binding target of stablilising greenhouse gas emissions to 1990 levels by 2000 (Brohe et al, 2009, 62; Schneider et al, 2010, 222). On the other hand, non-Annex 1 countries are developing countries that have typically contributed little to the problem, and have no emission reduction targets. Annex II countries are required to provide financial support to non-Annex I countries to combat climate change. This reflects the principles of equity and common but differentiated responsibilities set out in the Convention and indeed underlies much policy development of the era (Schneider et al, 2010, 222).

However, despite stating the need to stabilise emissions at a level that would prevent dangerous climate change, the UNFCCC did not specify what this level was, nor what the specific commitments of the convention were (Brohe et al, 2009, 62). The first Conference of Parties (often referred to as COP) was held in Berlin in 1995 and negotiations were held to develop more specific targets. By the third COP in 1997 in Japan, the Kyoto protocol was adopted, and came into force in 2005 (see Brohe et al, 2009; UNFCCC, 2012c; Schneider et al, 2010).

Kyoto protocol (adopted in 1997)

Box 4.2 provides a summary of the Kyoto Protocol. The key elements of the Protocol were that it defined binding emission reduction targets for 37 developed countries and the EU and also introduced emissions trading (UNFCCC, 2012c). Overall, the Kyoto targets 'add up to an average five per cent emissions reduction compared to 1990 levels over the five-year period 2008 to 2012' (UNFCCC, 2012c). The system introduced under Kyoto is usually referred to a 'cap and trade' system (for example, where emissions are both capped, and can be traded).

Box 4.2: Summary of the Kyoto protocol

Binding emissions reduction commitments for developed country parties

This acknowledged that the space to pollute was limited, and what is scarce and essential commands a price. GHG emissions, in particular carbon dioxide, became a new commodity. The Protocol began to internalise what is now recognised as an unpriced externality.

The flexible market mechanisms of the Protocol, based on the trade of emissions permits

Annex I Countries bound to the Protocol targets have to meet them mainly through domestic action. Part of these targets can be met through three market-based mechanisms that encourage GHG abatement where it is most cost-effective (for example, in the developing world). This has the additional benefit of stimulating green investment in developing countries and of including the private sector initiatives to reduce GHG emissions.
Source: UNFCCC, 2012c

There was some degree of flexibility within the Kyoto Protocol, enabling flexibility in *how* targets were met, allowing countries to 'bubble' their efforts and create flexible market mechanisms, for example, the EU chose to act as a whole under Kyoto (Schneider et al, 2010, 223). In addition, three market-based opportunities for emission reductions were introduced: international emissions trading, the clean development mechanism (CDM) which required investment in developing countries, or joint implementation (JI) which involved partnerships with other countries with emission reduction requirements (typically, this favoured investment in transition countries, most 'host' countries tended to be former Soviet states (UNFCCC, 2012e; Brohe et al, 2009, 97) (see Table 4.2)). In addition to these mechanisms, carbon credits were divided into four types:

Table 4.2: Features and examples of the additional mechanisms

Additional mechanisms	Features	Example
International emissions trading	'Emissions trading, as set out in Article 17 of the Kyoto Protocol, allows countries that have emission units to spare – emissions permitted them but not "used" – to sell this excess capacity to countries that are over their targets.' (UNFCCC, 2012f)	Many states (such as Canada and Japan) will meet their targets by purchasing AAUs from Russia and the Ukraine (Brohe et al, 2009, 101).
Joint implementation	'Defined in Article 6 of the Kyoto Protocol, allows a country with an emission reduction or limitation commitment under the Kyoto Protocol...to earn emission reduction units (ERUs) from an emission-reduction or emission removal project in another...Party, each equivalent to one tonne of CO2, which can be counted towards meeting its Kyoto target.' (UNFCCC, 2012f) It is important to stress that double counting must not occur (for example, that only the investor country, not the host country can claim the emission reductions)	Most ERUs were issued by Russia and the Ukraine in 2008, and tend to focus on energy (renewable, efficiency, fuel switching) (Brohe et al, 2009, 99).
Clean development mechanism	'Projects can earn saleable certified emission reduction (CER) credits, each equivalent to one tonne of CO2, which can be counted towards meeting Kyoto targets.' (UNFCCC, 2012f)	'A CDM project activity might involve, for example, a rural electrification project using solar panels or the installation of more energy-efficient boilers.' (UNFCCC, 2012f)

- Assigned amount units (AAUs), which are units of carbon that are permitted, but that will not be emitted by that country. These can be traded with countries that are less likely to meet their targets;
- Removal units (RMU) which are allocated on the basis of land use changes such as reforestation;
- Emission reduction units (ERUs) generated through joint implementation; and
- Certified emission reductions (CER) which are generated by CDM projects. (UNFCCC, 2012f)

There are a number of additional mechanisms that have developed as a result of the Kyoto Protocol. As described above, the EU opted to operate as a 'bubble', sharing emission reduction targets across member states. One of the most significant developments was the creation of the EU Emissions Trading Scheme in 2005 (EU ETS). The EU ETS has three phases (2005–07, 2008–12, 2013–20) which become more stringent over time. For example, the number of allowance allocations was significantly reduced between the first and second phase. The final phase will include aviation emissions, which were previously excluded (see Brohe et al, 2009).

Ratification of the Kyoto Protocol and 2012 onwards

International agreements can be fraught with conflict, especially given the problem of 'free riders'. While the Kyoto Protocol was ratified by most developed nations, a number of states delayed this process. For example, Australia ratified the Protocol in 2007 while the USA did not ratify the Protocol despite producing the greatest proportion of global emissions at the time, and in 2011 Canada revoked its ratification (EIA, 2012). Much debate about the ratification of the Protocol has been related to the definition of Annex I and non-Annex I countries. The justification for the withdrawal of Canada from the Kyoto Protocol was the exclusion of China (and other rapidly industrialised countries such as Brazil and India) from emission reduction commitments. The then Canadian Environment Minister Peter Kent explained the decision: 'The Kyoto Protocol does not cover the world's largest two emitters, United States and China, and therefore cannot work…It's now clear that Kyoto is not the path forward to a global solution to climate change. If anything it's an impediment' (CBS News, 2011).

Indeed, the 'free rider' problem (discussed in Chapter Five) has dominated climate change agreements, with China now emitting the most GHGs of any country, despite having no emission reduction commitments under the Kyoto protocol (EIA, 2012). However, to say that the failure of the US (and withdrawal of Canada) is simply an issue of fairness between countries is an over-simplification (see Chapter Five).

The period of the Kyoto Protocol came to an end in December 2012, and no replacement agreement has been made. The COP meetings: 2007 Bali (Indonesia), 2008 Poznan (Poland), 2009 Copenhagan (Denmark), 2010 Cancun (Mexico) and 2011 Durban (South Africa) have had limited success at developing a post-Kyoto agreement. This is despite the Bali Road map agreement two years previously that set out the need to come up with an agreement at the Copenhagan conference. Negotiations have tended to focus on whether countries such as China and India should be required to reduce emissions, or, whether the responsibilities negotiated under the Protocol should remain the same (see Bodansky, 2011). In 2011, parties at the Durban conference agreed to negotiate a new agreement by 2015. According to Bang et al (2012, 760) the EU persuaded other countries to commit to negotiation for a Protocol, or other legally binding instrument or agreed outcome by 2015. Box 4.3 reproduces the UNFCCC text highlighting what was agreed by the COP in Durban.

It is likely that a future agreement will focus on four elements: mitigation, adaptation, technology, and financing means of implementation and will include the development of a 'Green Climate Fund' which will support such activities in developing countries (Schneider et al, 2010, 230; UNFCCC, 2009, 4).

Many are optimistic that an agreement will be in place by 2015 while others see the delay as being detrimental to the climate policy process. For example, a spokesperson for International Greenpeace commented, 'Right now the global climate regime amounts to nothing more than a voluntary deal that's put off for a decade. This could take us over the 2°C threshold where we pass from danger to potential catastrophe' (BBC, 2011).

Box 4.3: UNFCCC text

Also decides to launch a process to develop a protocol, another legal instrument or an agreed outcome with legal force under the Convention applicable to all Parties, through a subsidiary body under the Convention hereby established and to be known as the Ad Hoc Working Group on the Durban Platform for Enhanced Action;

Further decides that the Ad Hoc Working Group on the Durban Platform for Enhanced Action; shall start its work as a matter of urgency in the first half of 2012 and shall report to future sessions of the Conference of the Parties on the progress of its work;

Decides that the Ad Hoc Working Group on the Durban Platform for Enhanced Action shall complete its work as early as possible, but no later than 2015 in order to adopt this protocol, legal instrument or agreed outcome with legal force at the twenty-first session.

Source: UNFCCC, 2011, 1

The role of the EU

Policy making also occurs at the 'supranational' level, most notably through the EU. The impact of the EU on environmental policy should not be underestimated, as it has implemented international decisions and encouraged action at the member state level which may not have been taken otherwise. Environmental policy was first introduced within the European Community (as it was then called) following the 1972 UN Stockholm Conference on the Human Environment with the first Environmental Action Plan (EAP) decided in 1973 (Hey, 2005, 19), and the second between 1977–81. While it is argued that successes were extremely limited, directives such as water and waste were developed during these years (Hey, 2005, 20). During the period 1982–7 discussions initially focused on the risks and benefits of environmental policies to the internal market (Hey, 2005, 20), and the need to harmonise environmental standards in order not to distort competitiveness. However, the rise in public environmental concern and success of green parties within mainstream politics led to a more ambitious approach between 1992–9 that had 'all the necessary elements of a policy oriented towards "ecological structural change"' (Hey, 2005, 23). The Maastricht treaty in 1993 introduced the word 'sustainable' into the formal aims of the EU, and 'continuous expansion' was replaced with 'sustainable and non-inflammatory growth respecting the environment' (Carter, 2007, 283). In 1999, in the Treaty of Amsterdam, the term 'sustainable development' was introduced, and environmental protection was sought across a range of policy areas (Carter, 2007, 283). While the momentum of the 1990s has arguably diminished (see Hey, 2005;or Carter, 2007), the legacy of these changes has had a significant impact on environmental policies, at the domestic and international level. As Home (2007, 7) explains, each EU member state commits to the *acquis communautaire* (the rights and obligations of EU membership, within which there are around 200 legal acts relating to the environment (*environmental acquis*). Countries wishing to join the EU must bring their laws in line with the *acquis communautaire* before they join (Home, 2007, 8). In many cases this requirement has led to an improvement in legislative and regulatory standards across Europe (Carter, 2007, 284).

Making and implementing environmental policies at the national level: policy instruments

Policy instruments are the tools that national governments use to achieve their policy objectives. There are four broad types of instrument: government expenditure, voluntary, economic or market-based instruments (MBIs), and regulation. The first three types of instrument are sometimes referred to as 'New Environmental Policy Instruments' (NEPIs) as their use at the national level was limited until the 1970s. The use of environmental policy instruments has changed significantly since the 1970s, moving away from a focus on a legalistic, regulatory approach, towards a greater use of economic instruments, voluntary agreements such as eco labels (Tews et al, 2003,

570). There has been a positive change in the number and diversity of policy instruments used even among countries that have previously been viewed as weak in terms of their environmental policies (Jordan et al, 2003b, 209). Table 4.3 provides an example of specific policy instruments in three different areas of environmental policy.

Expenditure

Governmental expenditure is one of the most basic policy instruments available to governments. By investing in particular technologies, developments or ideas, government can encourage growth in a particular area. For example, in 2012, despite much public debate, the UK government remained committed to subsidies promoting the development of wind farms, and more controversially nuclear energy (see Toke, 2011). The purpose of the wind farm subsidy is to support the growth of the renewable market in its infancy, with the ultimate aim of helping the UK to meet its domestic and international climate change policy commitments.

In addition to large-scale expenditure such as the subsidisation of particular industries, governmental expenditure has also been used to promote green 'messages' through education or informational campaigns. In the late 2000s the government commissioned a number of hard-hitting television, internet and poster commercials through the 'Act on CO_2' campaign (see Figure 4.1). These focused on the impacts of climate change and the need to take action immediately in order to protect future generations. In some instances the commercials attracted considerable numbers of complaints, both in terms of their terminology, and the use of fear tactics (see Guardian, 2010). The advertisements were (in)famous for their slant on fairy tale stories, use of child actors, and reworked nursery rhymes. Despite their controversy, the campaign won an award for being the best online green information campaign (see Charles, 2010).

Less controversially, spending in other areas has been used to encourage greener behaviour. In the late 2000s, the UK boiler

Table 4.3: Policy instruments and examples for three policy areas

	Transport	Waste disposal	Domestic energy
Expenditure	Public investment in 'green' infrastructure – for example, improving bus networks or train routes.	Public investment in recycling facilities, the provision of door step recycling, information campaigns encouraging greener behaviour such as the UK's Act on CO_2 campaign.	Public investment in housing stock to encourage energy efficiency, provision of free or cheap insulation, or boiler replacement schemes. The UK's 'warm front' scheme is a good example of public expenditure on domestic energy efficiency.
Voluntary	Encourage the creation of green travel plans in public and private organisations.	Encourage supermarkets to charge for non-recyclable plastic bags, or to promote recycling of unusual products such as batteries.	Encourage energy companies to explore alternative forms of energy.
Market-based instrument	Tax the most polluting forms of transport such as older vehicles or those that do a low millage per gallon, and reward the use of the cleanest forms such as highly efficient cars, and public transport.	Increase tax on non-recyclable materials, such as plastic bags, and reduce it on those that are recyclable.	Tax polluting forms of energy, provide incentives to use green energy, for example, in the UK the 'feed in' tariff pays householders to generate renewable energy.
Regulation	Set emissions standards. For example, in the UK environmental standards are enforced through the UK Ministry of Transport (MOT) test which is carried out on all vehicles that are three years old or more.	Set recycling quotas for local authorities, requiring them to recycle a certain percentage of domestic household waste (for example, in England in the early 2000s local authorities had a target of recycling 25 per cent of waste by 2005).	Ban particularly carbon intensive technologies, for example, the EU level ban on incandescent (traditional) light bulbs.

Figure 4.1: UK government awareness campaign poster

No one wants climate change,
least of all snowmen.

ACT ON
Save our climate for our children. Search online for **C** 2

replacement schemes encouraged energy efficiency improvements
(see Wallace et al, 2010). In addition, the publically funded Warm
Front scheme enabled low income households to access free energy
efficiency improvements such as new boilers and loft insulation and
promoted action where it would have been otherwise unaffordable.
The effectiveness of attempts to encourage individual level attitudinal
and behavioural change is discussed further in Chapter Five.

Regulation

Until the 1970s the most commonly used instrument at the national
level was regulation. Regulation provides governments with a way of
setting standards, and enforcing these with the threat of penalties for
non-compliance. There is still strong support for regulation in many
countries, as it forms a supporting function for other instruments,
helping to deal with point sources of pollution. It is also the main
instrument of EU environmental policy (Carter, 2007). However,
enforcement can be costly, as it requires both the monitoring of
pollution to assess compliance, and the expense of legal procedures in
the case of non-compliance. Also, in some cases, the penalties can be
ineffective, with polluters viewing fines or penalties of non-compliance
as a cheaper option than complying with regulations. Some argue that
regulations encourage certain companies or industries to move away
from countries with strict regulations (typically developed countries)

to those with weak environmental regulations or ability to ensure compliance (usually developing countries) called 'pollution havens'. Dean et al (2009) found that, in certain cases, investors are attracted by weak environmental standards

Market-based instruments

Japan introduced one of the first MBIs in 1974, Finland, other Nordic countries, Netherlands and France followed, with charges on water and air pollution. In contrast, the UK did not institute national environmental taxes until the mid-1990s. Use of MBIs has progressed, with hypothecation (ring-fencing revenue raised from economic instruments for use in environmental programmes) increasing in the 1990s and 2000s (see Carter, 2007). However, despite the increased popularity of MBIs among policy makers, it is likely that their use has been restricted by the lack of popularity among those affected by them. Tews et al (2003) note that 'the introduction of effective economic instruments regularly fails where powerful, well-organised economic interests are the potential losers in such a strategy. This is particularly true in the key fields for applying eco-taxes such as energy and transport (2003, 587). Indeed, a significant barrier to the use of MBIs is damage (or perceived damage) to economic competitiveness, especially where taxes are imposed on products or key factors of production where the goods are traded widely in the international market (OECD, 2002, 72). The perceived link between MBIs and decreased international competitiveness can lower their political feasibility. For example, both the Clinton administration's effort to introduce the 1993 energy tax and the Australian government's to introduce the 1994 Greenhouse Levy collapsed when energy intensive industries complained that they would be disadvantaged in the global market place (see Carter, 2007).

The issue of equity can also play a role in the development and use of MBIs. Tax increases on domestic fuel, food and other day-to-day necessities can have a disproportionate effect on those who can afford it the least (depending on the way in which the policy instruments are developed). In the UK for example, proposed increases in tax on domestic fuel failed due to the political outcry over the regressive distributional impact of the tax. As Gough (2012) suggests, 'any general carbon tax or pricing system would impact more on the low paid, single persons, pensioners and workless households', and unless these effects are factored into policy development, such policies are likely to be regressive.

Voluntary agreements

The popularity of voluntary agreements has grown significantly. Most agreements are voluntary and non-binding such as the EU Eco-Management and Auditing Scheme (EMAS) introduced in 1993. However, some states are experimenting with more formal and binding approaches known as negotiated agreements. These are contracts resulting from negotiations between public (national, federal or regional) authorities and industry, and their contents are defined jointly by industry and public bodies (Borkey and Leveque, 2000, 47). While the use of voluntary agreements has increased, where agreements are not binding they are often limited in their impact. One notable exception to this is the Forest Stewardship Council certification (FSC) label used in Sweden, the UK and a number of other countries (including Germany, Canada and Japan), where goods produced from sustainably managed forests are labelled to encourage customer awareness. As a result of the popularity of the FSC label, a change in some business activities has been observed (see Pattberg, 2005). The use of voluntary agreements has been favoured by business interests as it is a lighter touch than government regulation (Brouhle et al, 2009). In addition to this, certain certifications (for example, official fair trade or organic certifications) are regarded by business as a potential 'selling point', promoting a green, or ethical image, and appealing to environmentally conscious consumers (see Darnall et al, 2010; or Alberini and Segerson, 2002).

Policy instruments in developing countries and countries in transition

Given the importance of ensuring that development occurs sustainably within countries that are undergoing both industrial and political change, and the specific difficulties that such countries face when it comes to applying policy instruments, it is of value to consider them separately here. While there is limited academic literature on the design and implementation of policy instruments in developing countries and countries in transition, many of the factors discussed above are still applicable. Kathuria (2006, 406) argues that there are a number of factors that make the use of policy instruments more challenging:

> Developing countries and countries in transition often face more severe environmental degradation, a greater reliance on environmental resources for economic development, a weak institutional base to implement environmental policy, a greater risk of resistance to the introduction of MBIs, important issues of equity and social justice, and a weaker environmental research and development capacity.

There are two main points of view concerning the targeting of environmental problems in developing countries and countries in transition. One group (including organisations such as the World Bank) favour the use of market-based instruments as it is said to benefit:

- the treasury, through raised revenue;
- the environment, through encouraging polluters to change their behaviour and ploughing the money back into environmental initiatives;
- the economy, by encouraging private sector incentives. (Kathuria, 2006)

On the other hand, this approach is criticised by those who argue that greater consideration needs to be paid to specific national context, especially to financial, institutional and political factors. Such factors can make the use of regulation and market-based instruments more complex (and in some cases more problematic) than in industrialised countries for a number of reasons. First, the legal framework tends to mirror the state of economic development and therefore may limit the tax structure which an economy can bear (Backhaus, 2004, 1098). Second, the legal framework also limits a government's ability to regulate natural resource use by legal means, that is, to enforce regulations. Third, there may be a shortage of public officials, or poor pay and conditions, which may provide weak incentives for strict enforcement (O'Connor, 1998, 92). It is argued that in order for policy instruments to be effective in the context of developing countries and countries in transition, they must be supported by existing institutions – such as the legal system, levels of human capital and infrastructure – rather than exceeding institutional capacity. For example, the key ingredients that are said to be necessary for successful economic instruments – transparency, accurate monitoring, realistic incentive to trade and trust – are not always in place in developing countries and countries in transition. Backhaus (2004, 1098) argues that if economic instruments are to be used the 'approach has to be exceedingly simple, since both the number and quality of tax instruments available are limited'. Political support, along with that of the private sector, is also an essential ingredient in order to ensure both enforcement and compliance.

Understanding national level policy responses

The range of policy instruments used by different countries (and indeed in different sectors within countries) has expanded greatly with Jordan finding that:

> Some countries have adopted NEPIs much earlier (for certain sectors) than the rest. Also, NEPIs are often put to different tasks, voluntary agreements in the Netherlands tend to target processes and are mostly obligatory, whereas in Germany they tend to target products and are mostly legally non-binding. Also, the definitions of particular MBIs or voluntary agreements are very nation specific – one instrument in one country can differ greatly from the (apparently) same instrument used in another national context. For example, the German Environmental Expert

Council has argued that the UK's tradable permit scheme amounts to little more than a voluntary agreement combined with eco-taxes. (Jordan, 2003b, 212)

Investigating the use of NEPIs, Jordan et al (2003a) find that the increased use of these methods can be attributed to a number of factors:

1. dissatisfaction with regulation as a policy instrument;
2. the perceived strengths of alternative instruments;
3. the shift from government to governance;
4. a change of focus on instrument use in the EU;
5. economic pressures;
6. growing domestic political support.

There are a number of factors that influence the use of policy instruments (and indeed, the choice of instrument). At the global scale, international agreements and regimes produce policy frameworks, or legally binding targets (such as carbon emission targets) that force a national level policy response. Depending on the policy area and necessary policy outcomes some policy instruments will be more appropriate than others. Some international bodies such as the International Monetary Fund (IMF) that provide loans, may provide these with certain requirements such as structural adjustment programmes that favour the liberalisation of markets/reduction of state intervention. Naturally then, instruments based on strong state intervention may be sidelined in favour of MBIs. The EU, as a supranational organisation, imposes certain legal duties on member states. For example, the EU bathing water quality requirements has improved the quality of UK bathing water, while the EU level of carbon emissions targets have in part led to a range of policy measures including carbon pricing, governmental information campaigns and investment in green industries.

There are also social, economic, political and cultural explanations for the way in which policy instruments are used in different countries (see Jordan et al, 2002c; Connelly and Smith, 1999). National traditions and patterns of environmental management, such as the way in which different environmental issues are handled within government (usually across a range of different departments and policy levels) will affect responses. Typically, environmental concerns are a relatively low priority in liberal democracies, and environmental departments/ministries have a low status. Equally, existing policy networks (that is, the organisations and actors typically involved in decision-making processes) are likely to influence policy development and instrument use, for example where the private sector has a longstanding relationship with government, it may be likely that voluntary instruments are used in the first instance. Closely related is the national political system, for example, in Germany, due to its Additional Member System (AMS) electoral system that enables a degree of proportionality in its parliament, the Green Party has both won seats, and at times been part of a power sharing coalition, something that is highly unlikely under the UK 'first past the post' system (at the time of writing there is one Green Party MP in the House of Commons). The presence of Green Parties within government *may* lead to stronger and more decisive policies and policy instruments, although this varies vastly depending on the strength of the coalition, coalition agreement among other things. Clearly, the ideological position of the government will also play a role in the development of policy and policy instruments, for example, Bang et al (2012) discuss the ideological opposition to international climate policies in the US.

Cultural factors also influence the development of policy, where different environmental, geographic and social histories may shape national priorities. For example, the UK has a strong history of animal welfare and nature conservation compared to many countries (see White et al, 2011), whereas policy in countries such as Sweden have had to respond to specific environmental problems such as acid rain.

SUMMARY

- Resolving environmental problems that cross national boundaries requires international action.
- Given an absence of a global government, international environmental action is usually undertaken through the development of international regimes.
- Climate policy is a good example of an international regime in action and highlights the wide range of actors involved and the complexity of the negotiations.
- At the national level there are four main instruments that can be used to implement environmental policies: expenditure, regulation, market-based instruments and voluntary measures.
- Expenditure refers to government spending and investment, often in new technologies or educational campaigns.
- Regulation refers to setting environmental standards, and applying penalties where these are breached.
- Market-based instruments are often referred to as 'carrot and stick' measures. Typically the taxation system is used to penalise environmentally polluting activities, and to reward 'green' activities.
- Voluntary agreements are often associated with voluntary action often used by companies to improve their environmental credentials.
- The implementation of policy instruments varies by country, and is dependent on a number of factors.

READING GUIDE

Brohe, A, Eyre, N, Howarth, N, 2009, *Carbon markets: An international business guide*, London: Earthscan

Carter, N, 2007, *The politics of the environment*, 2nd edn, Cambridge: Cambridge University Press

Downie, D, 2011, Global environmental policy: Governance through regimes, in RS Axelrod, SD VanDeveer, DL Downie (eds) *The global environment: Institutions, law and policy*, Washington, DC: CQ Press

Jordan, A, Adelle, C, 2012, Environmental policy in the European Union: Contexts, actors and policy dynamics, 3rd edn, London and Sterling, VA: Routledge

Jordan, A, Wurzel, RKW, Zito, AR, 2003a, 'New' instruments of environmental governance: Patterns and pathways of change, *Environmental Politics* 12, 1, 3–24

5

Environmental policy challenges

Introduction

Environmental policy varies significantly at the international, supranational, national, and local level. There are a number of factors which influence the way in which environmental policies are shaped, and may also explain why they sometimes fail. This chapter considers the main barriers, problems and challenges associated with policy making at a range of levels. Before considering specific policy levels, the chapter discusses two factors that underlie all forms of decision-making: the limitations of sustainable development and ecological modernisation, and the role of science and evidence in decision-making.

Underlying issues

The limitations of sustainable development

Sustainable development has largely been viewed as the dominant policy approach to environmental problems as it offers the possibility of economic development while protecting the environment (see Chapter One). The concept of sustainable development has been adopted by governments, industry and NGOs. One of the reasons for its widespread appeal is that it does not necessarily challenge the predominant liberal economic paradigm which sees a free market and economic growth as essential for human welfare. The strength of the concept is in that it can often bring opposing groups together, but at the same time its vagueness means that policies that actually achieve sustainable development in practice are rare.

While the 'Brundtland' definition is the most commonly accepted definition of sustainable development, there are different approaches to achieving it. The 'techno-centric' approach sees technology and science as providing the solutions to environmental problems that threaten human wellbeing. In contrast, the 'eco-centric' approach emphasises the need for radical change in political structures and human life (Sharp, 1999). However, common principles include maintaining the resource base, equity for current and future generations, and the need to achieve not only ecological but also social and economic sustainability within the ecological limits. The ambiguity in the Brundtland Commission's definition of sustainable development has led to weak and strong interpretations. *Weak sustainability* allows for substitution between different types of capital assets. For example, technological developments can be substituted for natural resources so that we leave future generations not with the natural resource but with the ability to live without it. Proponents of *strong sustainability* argue that in most cases natural resources cannot be substituted and any use of a resource needs to be accompanied by a restoration process (for example, reforestation). The deep ecology view of sustainable development, for example, involves social and political restructuring and redistribution that reduces consumption and prevents the need for economic growth (Carter, 2007, 207–38).

In his critical review of sustainable development, Lele suggested that 'sustainable development is a "metafix" that will unite everybody from the profit-minded industrialist and risk-minimising subsistence farmer to the equity-seeking social worker, the pollution-concerned or wildlife-loving first worlder, the growth-maximising policymaker, the goal-orientated bureaucrat, and, therefore, the vote-counting politician' (1991, 613). He goes on to argue that the process of sustainable development has hardly begun, with the technocentric approach still dominant even in sustainable development discourse, with few challenges to deeper socio-political or cultural values (Lele, 1991). In addition to this argument, there is little consensus on what are desirable outcomes under sustainable development or how those desirable outcomes might be achieved. The contested nature of sustainable development presents particular problems for the legitimacy of any policy process that claims to be driven by sustainable development principles.

There are those who feel that policy made under the banner of sustainable development does not do enough to tackle the conflicts and tensions between environmental, social and economic goals. For example, Luke (2005, 28) questions sustainable development as an ideological construct arguing that the term 'is increasingly used as a label to place over modes of existence that are neither sustainable nor development'.

The limitations of ecological modernisation

Described by some as a 'weak' expression of sustainable development, ecological modernisation also has a number of problems. It is limited to activities where technology can supply solutions; it assumes that market criteria can be applied to all environmental problems; it does not attempt to deal with inequalities; and perhaps, what is most important, it assumes that consumption can continue to increase unabated. Ecological modernisation has its roots in the developed countries of Western Europe and it is in countries such as Germany and the Netherlands where it has seen most success. Even here, however, the evidence for the effectiveness of ecological modernisation is limited, while in industry it is practically non-existent (Carter, 2007, 233). In government, unsuitable political systems, a reluctance to change traditional policy responses, and an active opposition by state institutions, have hindered the uptake of ecological modernisation. In industry, a lack of knowledge and the costs of change both serve to limit the effective implementation of ecological modernisation in the business sector.

The relationship between science, society and policy

Scientific evidence plays a key role in policy decision-making. However, there can be a significant gap between science and policy, something that is exacerbated by different disciplinary cultures, terminology, and understandings (see Chapter Three). Science has become increasingly challenged in the public sphere. For example, with regard to biotechnology, in the 1970s the public were regarded as the 'audience' of science. Then biotechnology was a technical concept, self-regulating and a provider of knowledge to society (Abels, 2005). Over the following decades, this view shifted as biotechnology became increasingly regulated by policy makers, and public concerns regarding safety were more fully integrated into decision making.

How science is communicated to the public and policy makers is also important. Some argue that science communication is rarely neutral (Hulme, 2009), and that policy makers and the media 'frame' science when communicating with the public. That is, they present evidence in a particular way, or present particular forms of evidence to convey a particular idea or message. For example, climate change messages may be presented in particular ways (in the media, by politicians and other organisations and actors), with some focusing on the image of a polar bear stranded on an iceberg in order to appeal to the hearts and minds of animal lovers; others focusing on the uncertainty of science to appeal to climate sceptics; and some using a 'catastrophe' frame to describe the dire consequences of inaction. An extreme example of the catastrophe/danger frame is Greenpeace's framing of the negative effects of genetic modification (GM) in the 1990s, which indicated the possible horrors of consuming GM foods.

The problem with the relationship between science, scientists and policy makers lies in what science can and cannot provide. Oreskes (2004, 369) suggests that,

> We all want our views to be based on truth, many of us look to science to provide truth. The truth is not always convenient, however, and it is rarely convenient for everyone, generating the incentive for manipulation and misrepresentation of information. This is particularly true in the domain of environmental policy.

Discussions of risk are central to such debates, where policy makers must weigh up a range of evidence, and consider the social, economic and environment costs and benefits of different policy options including taking no action. Decisions about risk are plagued by issues of uncertainty, gaps in understanding, inaccuracies in existing knowledge and inderterminancy (that is, where issues are new and novel and so outcomes are impossible to know for certain) (Willows and Connell, 2003, 43; Bingham and Blackmore, 2003, 128).

Given these issues, the precautionary principle has become mainstream in environmental thought where a 'lack of full scientific certainty shall not be used as a reason for postponing cost-effective measures to prevent environmental degradation' (UNCED, 1992b) (see Chapter One). In reality, scientific uncertainty and doubt have fed political agendas. Indeed, scientific understandings are often uncertain or diverse enough to justify a range of competing political agendas, for example, the Bush administration was criticised for using 'unrepresentative and poorly supported' findings to support its climate policy (Pielke, 2004; Higgins et al, 2006).

International issues

At the international level countries often have conflicting interests which reduce the incentive to work collectively. Since no nation state can be excluded from the global commons (that is, oceans and atmosphere) some states will free-ride on the efforts of others. Chasek et al (2006, 198) identified four key interrelated obstacles to strong environmental regimes:

1. obstacles characteristic of environmental problems
2. a lack of necessary and sufficient conditions
3. systemic or structural obstacles
4. procedural obstacles related to negotiations.

Some of these issues are now considered in more depth within the context of climate change.

Obstacles characteristic of environmental problems

Environmental damage creates a unique policy problem, given its effects across time and space (Chasek et al, 2006, 204–8). A number of related factors weaken policy making and implementation. First is the issue of scientific uncertainty, which can have a significant impact on international policy responses. Climate change is a key example of this where, despite a scientific consensus supporting the existing of human-induced climate change, issues of uncertainty and the need for more conclusive research prior to any action are still arguments made by some states as reasons to delay action (Hulme, 2010).

Also, the source of environmental problems, the location where they are felt the worst, and the most appropriate location for policy measures may not be the same, or map neatly along national borders. As a result, the impacts of policy interventions have the potential to be unequally distributed, determined by geographic and environmental factors, rather than by a country's ability to pay or its contribution to the problem. For example, some climate change mechanisms promote the prevention of deforestation in developing countries, and without incentives or redistributive efforts the costs of these policies may fall disproportionately on those who cannot afford it.

Necessary and sufficient conditions

Strong regimes require sufficient concern about the environmental problem in question and the capacity to act (Chasek et al, 2006). Nation states first have to agree that there is an environmental problem that requires international agreement (Castells and Ravetz, 2001, 405). In addition, solutions need to be identifiable and feasible. Science and the precautionary principle play a key role in determining the causes and possible solutions. However, solutions need to be economically viable if nations are to agree to their implementation.

The ability to implement and enforce agreements is also regarded as essential to regime success. Clearly there is limited value in imposing carbon emission reduction targets on a country if it does not have the capacity to meet the targets. A nation's ability to act must be considered during international negotiations. This is why a focus has been placed on financial support and technology transfer to developing countries during climate discussions. However, even if a nation is technically and economically able to implement measures, this does not guarantee its support for them, or indeed compliance. Numerous domestic political factors may inhibit the adoption and/ or implementation of environmental agreements. Decisions within developed countries have been criticised for being driven by political short-termism and a preference for technical 'end of pipe' solutions rather than addressing broader changes to production and consumption and ecological vulnerability (Pelletier, 2010). Kelemen and Vogel (2010, 434–5) state that:

> [W]hen environmental pressure groups and green parties are relatively weak, domestic political support for international environmental agreements also weakens. Where domestic environmental forces are weaker and domestic standards more lax, domestic firms and governments have an economic interest in opposing international agreements that would force them to raise domestic standards.

As highlighted above, compliance is a significant issue within international regimes, and there is often limited capacity to monitor and enforce particular agreed environmental standards or limits. Therefore there is a temptation for participating countries not to fulfil their commitments, especially if it appears not to be in the national interest (Lidskog and Sundquvist, 2002, 79; Hovi et al, 2009, 31).

Systemic or structural obstacles

There are a broad range of systemic or structural obstacles to the development of strong international regimes (Chasek et al, 2006, 198–201). Many of these relate to arguments about fairness and include: strong states attempting to dominate weak states, national concern about unfair economic or political advantages, national concern regarding non-compliance elsewhere, problems of sovereignty (action within one country can damage the environment in another) and the role of international economic systems (with a focus on lowest cost production). Hovi et al (2009) describes the international policy environment as one of anarchy. Many argue that international regimes are highly limited in terms of their decision-making and enforcement powers, where the reliance on their 'traditional foundations: self-interest, reciprocity, and consent' is considered a weakness (Bodansky, 1999, 600). Equally, regimes are highly fragile and vulnerable to change. Levy et al (1994, 17) suggests one school of thought '[that] specific regimes will be abandoned when the underlying power distribution changes or when institutional commitments become inconvenient to one or more powerful member states'. In the context of climate change negotiations, a number of collective action problems that limit effective agreements can be outlined:

■ The benefits of reduced global warming accrue to all countries, not only those that reduce their emissions of greenhouse gases. There is a temptation for each country to leave a disproportionate share of the mitigation burden to others.
■ Some countries might be tempted to decline to participate and 'free-ride' on the efforts of other nation states.
■ In multilateral environmental regimes, punishing non-compliance is costly, with costs falling on countries that are already in compliance. The incentive to punish is thus weaker.
■ For several countries, fulfilling their greenhouse gas targets will entail significant costs. Indeed, the expected damage to its economy was one of the major reasons why the US declined to ratify the Kyoto Protocol to combat climate change reduce greenhouse gases in 2001. (Hovi et al, 2009, 30–2)

National interests and concerns about economic fairness dominate international negotiations, both from developed and developing country perspectives. Roberts and Parks (2007, 3) highlight:

President Bill Clinton signed on to the Kyoto Protocol…but even before he did the US Senate voted 95 to 0…[to] block any 'unfair' treaty that did not require the poor nations to also address the problem. This move by the US bred great animosity in the developing world.

Many developing countries have contributed little to the greenhouse gas emissions responsible for climate change. In addition, they can lack the capacity to implement solutions and are often the least influential within international decision-making processes. Historically, developing countries have regarded international regimes with suspicion; viewing them as a means of controlling resources and preventing development (Snell and Quinn, 2011; Chasek et al, 2006). Following the publication of the 2006 Stern review of the economics of climate change, Sir Nicholas Stern reiterated the importance of the fairness, and support for developing countries within climate negotiations:

If the rich world were to emit zero in 2050, the countries currently seen as 'developing', 8 billion out of the 9 billion, would have to have an average of 2.5 tonnes per capita by 2050 for the 20Gt CO_2 flow of emissions to be achieved. They are least responsible for the bad starting point and earliest and hardest hit. It is for them to set out the overall terms of a global deal and to place the necessary conditionalities on the rich world: strong targets, early demonstration of low carbon growth, carbon finance, sharing of technology and strong assistance with funding for adaption. (Stern writing in Brohe et al, 2009, xv)

Climate negotiations have significantly faltered over discussions of whether countries such as China and India should be allowed to continue to emit greenhouse gasses with no limits (see Chapter Four). Equally, whether developing countries should face any cap in emissions, and if alternative development trajectories will be supported through financial mechanisms (such as the CDM), the value of these mechanisms continue to dominate climate negotiations.

Procedural obstacles related to negotiations

In addition to the difficulties of coming to an agreement, the effectiveness of agreements can also be questionable as agreements are often politically driven rather than grounded in scientific evidence. As Pelletier (2010, 221) suggests 'emission reductions are only effective if they are sufficient to achieve environmental improvement'. He argues that:

> [T]he focus is on politically expedient rather than environmentally realistic reduction targets and technological solutions that do little to reduce fossil energy dependency. Even more insidious, however, is that the Protocol actually serves to perpetuate expansionary and energy-intensive development through the Clean Development Mechanism (CDM). (Pelletier, 2010, 221)

As suggested by Pelletier, the decisions and to some extent the compromises made in the negotiations of the Kyoto Protocol have been subjected to significant criticism. For example, Brohe et al (2009, 103) highlight the criticisms around the integrity of the carbon market developed under Kyoto, commenting that allocations favoured the former Eastern bloc (Russia, Ukraine, Bulgaria and Romania), enabling them to sell emission credits, despite achieving no domestic emission reductions. Equally, the CDM has been criticised in terms of its lack of support for new technologies, the types of projects included (and excluded), the location of projects, and implementation costs (Brohe et al, 2009, 90–3). More broadly, the CDM performs as a market where the cheapest carbon credits are sought and this does not necessarily support broader aims such as sustainable development within developing countries, and is at best carbon neutral (Brohe, 2009; Snell and Quinn, 2011).

As a result of many of the factors described above, the process of negotiating an agreement is time consuming and lengthy. At the time of writing the Kyoto greenhouse gas emissions commitments will end, and post 2012 there will be no targets in place until these are negotiated despite the numerous attempts to set targets (see Chapter

Four). Given that climate negotiations have been in place since 1995, progress towards combating climate change has been described by some as highly limited.

National issues

Any policy decision needs to be understood in terms of the context in which it operates. Globalisation, decisions in other policy areas, economic factors, and prevailing political ideologies all shape national policy (Roberts, 2011, 146). As Hill (2009, 109) suggests:

> There is a need not to forget the complexity of modern governance. This means that institutions of government may be international, that groups may be organised outside and across individual states, that issues about inequalities of power need to be analysed globally, and that choices are made by actors who are increasingly conscious that they are playing on an international stage.

There are both external influences on national policy development as well as internal drivers. The next section will briefly consider a number of theories that attempt to explain the role of power, institutions, history and policy change in influencing the formulation and implementation of policy.

The influence of international processes, organisations and institutions

In addition to international agreements such as a ban on whaling or national greenhouse emission reduction targets, the extent to which a country is integrated into a supranational organisation may also have an impact on national policy development (Knill et al, 2010, 302). Indeed, as described in Chapter Four, any consideration of domestic policy making among EU member states must consider the influence that the EU has on policy development and implementation (Lowe and Ward, 1998).

International and supranational institutions can influence and shape national policy development and implementation. Policy convergence is one of the central ideas in this area, and describes the adoption of similar policies across countries. Busch and Jörgens (2005) describe a typology to explain how policy convergence occurs (see Table 5.1). Leaving aside coercion (which refers to policy developments that are imposed on a country regardless of their support for them, or

Table 5.1: Mechanisms for policy convergence

Mechanism	IMPOSITION	HARMONIZATION	DIFFUSION
Mode of operation	Coercion, political or economic conditionality Decentralised decision-making	Negotiation, enforcement and monitoring Centralised and joint decision-making	Persuasion, emulation and learning Decentralised decision-making
Principal motivations of national policy makers to adopt external policy models	Export fundamental values and principles as well as policies perceived to be successful Access to economic and political resources (for example, join international decision-making bodies or gain financial support) Avoid negative consequences (for example, sanctions)	Manage effectively transboundary challenges and at the same time dissatisfaction with solutions to transboundary challenges provided for by unilateral action Avoid negative externalities (for example, trade distortions) Realise positive gains (for example, access to new markets)	Search for effective solutions for domestic problems Gain internal and external legitimacy
Degree of influence on design of policy innovation and decision to adopt it	Low		High

Source: Busch and Jörgens, 2005, 867

role within policy negotiations), the most relevant explanations of convergence are harmonisation and diffusion. Harmonisation within the context of environmental policy suggests that as international (or supranational) agreements are made, countries have to alter domestic policy in order to meet specified targets or commitments. Countries that have similar commitments are likely to move in a similar policy trajectory (for example, they all take action to reduce national carbon emissions). Policy diffusion refers largely to processes of policy transfer, where countries imitate, emulate and learn from the policy-making process in other countries (Busch and Jörgens, 2005, 865).

Domestic factors

In addition to international and supranational influences, national decision-making can be highly complex and variable. Many national governments established environment ministries to tackle environmental issues as a response to rising environmental awareness and public concern that emerged in the 1970s. However, environmental policies often require the integration of policy across sectors *within* national governments if they are to be successfully integrated into national policy. There are so many varieties of national practice that it is difficult to categorise these in terms of their environmental policy activities. Wells (1995, 24) identifies three general types of policy practice:

- a centralised agency with general jurisdiction for environmental policy usually found in countries with unitary systems of government;
- decentralised responsibilities with environmental policy responsibilities at the provincial or regional level, largely associated with weak states;
- federal systems where environmental policy responsibilities are distributed across central and state governments.

Understanding how domestic policies are developed and implemented is a huge task, and an entire academic field is dedicated to this, with numerous theories that attempt to describe and explain the policy process. Even within the environmental policy literature understanding of policy making vary widely, both by theoretical approach, and by sector (see Roberts, 2011). In essence discussions about the policy making process tend to focus on two core elements; how policies are shaped, and how decisions come to be made (Hill, 2009), and these are now discussed below.

Explaining how policies are shaped

There are many theories that attempt to understand and categorise decision-making. One of the key areas of interest is how issues and interests make the political agenda (and how they do not). Writers in this area discuss the distribution of power within the policy process, and the most notable theories include pluralism, corporatism and elitism.

At its purest level, pluralism suggests that no group is without power to influence decision-making, but equally no group is dominant. Any group can ensure that its political preferences and wishes are adopted if it is sufficiently determined (Hill, 2009, 28). Under this understanding, no interests are actively excluded (Roberts, 2011, 154). Hill argues that pluralist arguments have developed and been revised, first to consider 'democratic elitism', and second, to propose alternatives to pluralist theories through structuralist arguments. Within democratic systems elitist theories focus on political elitism, through the 'growth of large firms, the establishment of trade unions and development of political parties' (Roberts, 2011, 38). However, interest has also grown in corporatist theory, that considers how competition between national economies, concentrations of ownership and changes in economic systems have prompted the shift towards corporatism, where trade unions and economic interests are both brought into a relationship with the state. Hill (2009, 54) argues that corporatism in this form has largely replaced pluralist understandings of power relations.

However, corporatist theories have been criticised for being too simplistic in their description of policy development given their focus on the relationship between state, labour and capital. As a result, more subtle ways of understanding the relationship between state and other interests have emerged. The most significant theoretical development in this field is policy network analysis and its focus on policy communities and issue networks. Policy network analysis is usually situated within the context of discussions around governance and the 'hollowing out' of the state (Hudson and Lowe, 2009). Policy network analysis considers the numerous organisations and institutions involved in decision-making. It attempts to conceptualise these relationships, particularly considering the role of policy communities and issue networks. While a policy community is said to have a relative power balance, an exchange of resources, and shared values, the looser issue network is large, has much lower levels of agreement, unequal power, and is less likely to be able to coordinate itself. Hill (2009, 58–9) gives the example of the changing nature of British agricultural policy. From the 1940s to the 1970s this was a close knit policy community made up of landowners, farmers, the appropriate government department, and fertiliser industry. However, from the 1980s onwards it moved to a more diffuse issue network considering of a number of governmental departments, environmental groups, and consumer interests. As such, policy network analysis enables us to consider where governmental environmental ministries and bureaucratic departments sit within decision-making processes, and whether they might be considered central or indeed peripheral to environment-related decisions.

In addition to understanding environmental decision-making policy, network analysis also enables us to think more broadly about policy development. Policy does not operate in a vacuum, and actors that may be central players in policy communities, may sit on the peripheries of issue networks in other policy spheres. This is particularly important given that environmental concerns encompass many policy areas (for example, business, transport, food and agriculture, science and technology), and problems generally cannot be resolved without some degree of integration with other policy areas. When environmental ministries or departments have a limited role within the policy this may result in limited environmental policies.

Explaining how policies are made

While the theories described above consider relationships between policy actors and the balance of power, a number of other theoretical approaches attempt to explain policy stability and policy change. Hill (2009, 82) suggests 'it is implicit in institutional theories that if countries differ because of their different institutional configurations then their policy processes are likely to differ'. Institutional theories emphasise 'constraints on change and pathways that change may follow' (Hill, 2009, 76). Much institutional theory focuses on the stability that institutions lend to policy making, often leading to incremental policy changes, or resistance to change, rather than large step changes. Knill et al (2010, 306) investigated a number of factors claimed to affect OECD environmental policy development. They suggest that: 'Consensual institutions – for example, proportional electoral systems resulting in multi-party legislatures, (broad) coalitions and collegial executives – have a greater capacity to represent diffuse groups (including environmental interests) and are less susceptible to the influence of special interest groups.'

Considering the domestic factors that prevented the US ratification of Kyoto, Bang et al (2012, 757) draw attention to the role of the American political system, highlighting the impact of the federal system where senators are found to defend constituency interests over party interests. Similarly, Konig and Luetgert (2008) examined the delays by EU Member States in ratifying EU environment-related directives and suggest that 'Lijphart's federalism...[is] significant and positively correlated with delay' as is the complexity of institutional arrangements (2008, 189,191). Similarly, Wurzel (2010, 467) comments on some of the 'structural constraints' of the German political system:

> In the past Germany often had great difficulties to present a well co-ordinated national position in EU negotiations because of key institutional features of the German political system which is characterised by a relatively high degree of ministerial independence, underdeveloped interdepartmental co-ordination, coalition government and a federal

system in which environmental policy competences are split between
the federal government and the states.

However it must be noted that whilst institutional arrangements clearly
shape domestic choices, the exact nature of this effect is unclear.

Those arguing from an institutional perspective often discuss the
concept of 'path dependency', described by Greener (2005, 62)
as 'choices formed when an institution is being formed, or when a
policy is being formulated, have a constraining effect into the future'.
Considering specific changes in the direction of environmental policy in
Germany, Wurzel (2010, 475) finds that 'The Grand Coalition's ability
to induce...change has been constrained by a "dual path dependency"',
given the largely consensual approach to environmental issues within
Germany since the 1960s and restrictions imposed by existing policy
commitments.

Theory in this area also considers how the policy-making process
results in particular environmental issues reaching the political, and
policy agenda. Rational models of decision-making suggest that policy
makers select policy goals, they are then are presented with a number
of solutions and select and implement the most effective solution
(see Simon, 1957). However, critics of this approach such as Charles
Lindblom propose that in reality policies represent (and indeed should
represent) small step changes in existing policy (see Hill, 2009, 153–4).
Incrementalist explanations, it is argued, more appropriately explain
the changing nature of policy problems, and the fragmented policy
environment compared to rational choice theories (Snellen and van
de Donk, 1998, 385).

However, policies do change, and sometimes changes may, at least on
the surface, appear dramatic and rapid. Baumgartner and Jones (1993)
suggest the idea of 'punctuated equilibrium' as one way of understanding
how change occurs. They argue that while policy is characterised by
periods of stability, consensus, and incremental change, when new
issues emerge they can lead to brief periods of rapid change, both
in terms of policy and also institutions, before stabilising once more

(Parsons, 1995, 203–4). They argue that punctuated equilibrium is driven by two interrelated factors: policy image and portrayal, and the institutional context that the issues sit within (Parsons, 1995, 203–4). Punctuated equilibrium has been used by policy analysts to explain changes in a number of different types of policy area, environmental policy lending itself particularly to such theories given the nature and visibility of some large scale environmental events (such as natural disasters or human caused forms of pollution such as oil spills). The idea fits closely to the issue attention cycle as well, given the visibility of environmental problems, and fluctuating media and public interest in them. This is of course just one attempt to explain policy change, and those interested in policy analysis should consult the texts identified at the end of this chapter. However, one message implicit in any theory of policy change is the role of exogenous factors. Carter (2007, 197) identifies five specific exogenous factors that may accelerate environmental policy making:

- a sudden crisis (for example, BSE crisis in the 1990s)
- a new problem (for example, emergence of climate change as an issue)
- changes in external relations – for example, EU regulations or international agreements
- emergence of new social movements or pressure groups
- action by political actors to break up a policy community.

Box 5.1 presents a case study of UK climate policy. It shows how support for the Stern review on climate change at its inception, public concern, changes within industry, and international pressures may have all supported further development of climate policy.

Box 5.1: Climate policy in 2006 in the UK – policy change?

Considering the 'backstory' to UK climate politics Jordan and Lorenzoni (2007) identify a complex policy background. The 2006 Stern review on the economics of climate change was published at a time where political attention was already focused on concerns about energy security, public concern about climate change was at a high, and a number of large companies and the three main political parties announced their 'pro- environmental' credentials (Jordan and Lorenzoni, 2007, 312–13). In addition, a number of 'new' policy instruments had been introduced after the Labour Party took office in 1997, including the Climate Change Levy (a tax on non-domestic energy) that is likely to have acted as an incentive for industry to address energy efficiency.

In addition to the Stern review, the UK government published the '2006 UK climate change programme' and the Climate Bill in 2007 which eventually became the 2008 Climate Change Act. The Act outlined legally binding targets for reducing greenhouse gas emissions by 80 per cent by 2050 (Snell, 2008). In addition to this, the 2007 UK Energy Efficiency Action Plan was published alongside the Green Paper for more sustainable and affordable homes and the 2006 Energy review (Snell, 2008).

Jordan and Lorenzoni suggest two significant factors may have supported the favourable response to the Stern Review (and climate change more generally). First, they argue that 'the messenger was different', rather than the review being commissioned by an external organisation (such as an environmental charity) or even a governmental environment ministry, it was commissioned by the then Chancellor of the Exchequer, Gordon Brown, and was supported by the Prime Minister, Tony Blair (Jordan and Lorenzoni, 2007, 317). Second, they argue that 'the audience in both the public and private spheres was politically more attuned to what [Stern] had to say' (Jordan and Lorenzoni, 2007, 317).

Local issues

At the local level there are a number of factors that shape the integration of environmental concerns into local policy. These factors mean that policy development, outputs and outcomes are often significantly different between different administrative areas in the same country with the nature, remit and role of local government varying widely between countries. This section introduces some of the issues commonly associated with local politics and policy, using the UK as an example.

Explaining local decision-making

First, the remit of local government has an impact on the scope and extent of policy development. Notions of the competition state and the shift from government to governance are useful in understanding changes at the local government level, where a reduction in local government duties (and in some instances powers) in favour of the private and/or voluntary sector is increasingly common. For example, since the privatisation of most UK bus services in the 1980s, English local government transport departments no longer have direct control over these services.

Second, policies can be shaped by the way in which local government is organised. In the UK, there are currently two main types of authority: two-tier authorities and unitary authorities. In the two-tier system, the larger scale county level has control over the setting of policy areas such as transport, whereas the smaller scale district or borough level has control over issues relating to planning. If the county and district do not work collaboratively then policy development can be hampered. Where countries have regional levels of government (recently abolished in the UK) with different administrative duties this can also make policy development more complex.

Third, and closely related, policy making at the local level is traditionally compartmentalised, and is generally developed around the provision of key services. At the local level, environmental issues are largely placed within environmental health or planning departments and are subject to competing interests, such as a variety of environmental pressure groups, economic and commercial interests. The make-up of the local authority can have an important impact on policy development. The focus and remit of different departments within the local authority may determine the focus and remit of policy development. For example, Snell (2009) finds that where sustainable development responsibilities are located within a regeneration and development department, the resulting policies have a very different focus from those emerging from an environment department responsibilities. As described in previous chapters, typically, thinking concerning environmental policy responses has become more holistic, requiring a combination of economic, social and environmental concerns, which may not sit easily with compartmentalised systems of local government. For example, in the mid-2000s, the English government introduced 'accessibility planning', a form of transport planning that required inter-departmental cooperation in order to consider a range of needs and concerns in the making of transport provision. This type of policy suffered as a result of the differences between disciplines, policy officers with different sectoral backgrounds (for example, social work, education, children and young people, environmental management, planning, engineering and so on), physical locations of different departments, and different stakeholder procedures. Equally, the trend towards ecological modernisation (see Chapter One) places environmental concerns and duties into departments and organisations with no historical remit or disciplinary background.

Fourth, policy networks can have a significant impact on local policy development, and can be associated with limiting the extent to which concern for the environment drives local policy making. Traditionally economic interests are dominant at the local level, and it can be difficult to overcome these. Chatterton and Style (2001, 226) argue that the 'traditional ground for local policy networks has been economic development in which environmental concerns and sustainable development play a peripheral part'. Fifth, local politics and political campaigns also have an impact on policy development. Local politicians may be unwilling to appear to make extreme choices (for example, introducing a road congestion charge) especially if an election is imminent. This can also have the reverse effect. If the local area suffers from a particular problem that is felt at the local level (that is, extreme congestion, high numbers of pedestrian road deaths, air pollution, erosion of the local landscape) these may become a political priority. High-level local political support (or lack thereof) will determine in part how successfully environmental concerns are integrated into local policy making.

The introduction of a congestion charge in central London is an example of these factors in action. While in many cases these can militate against change, they can also drive it. According to Rye et al, 'London is the first big western city to have implemented a congestion charging scheme. The idea has been floating for decades but no one anywhere had dared to implement a policy that could encounter strong public opposition' (2003, 13). Box 5.2 outlines the reasons the authors believe the charge was implemented.

Box 5.2: Explaining the introduction of the congestion charge in London

The remit of the agency implementing the congestion charge – Transport for London (TfL) – is broader than that of other local authorities in the UK (and Western Europe). TfL has responsibility for major roads, buses, light rail and the underground system; TfL is also responsible for implementing the congestion charge. This is atypical, as other local authorities have no direct control over the bus network, and would be dependent on private bus operators to deliver improved public transport alongside a congestion-charging scheme.

Political powers in London are also different from those of other administrative areas in England. Policy-makers in London were able to place a levy on the council tax (the tax paid to the local authority by each household). As a result, relatively high levels of resources were deployed for both the development and implementation of the congestion charge, and these are said to have contributed towards its success. As most English local authorities do not have the power to make such changes they are usually more dependent on national or EU funding, or funding via public–private partnerships (which could make the scheme more controversial). Also, the structure of local government in London means that resources are not focused on particular geographic areas, and instead policy decisions rest centrally with the Mayor of London.

Finally, the policy problem has been defined as one as relating to the economy, health, and quality of life, rather than simply to transport. This has meant that congestion hasn't been 'compartmentalised' as a transport issue, and therefore that it has been presented to members of the public and various stakeholders in a way that is more politically acceptable. Indeed, the then Mayor of London, Ken Livingston, was elected despite his promise to bring in a congestion charge. While there has been opposition to the congestion charge, the strong pro-congestion charge policy community has never been sufficiently penetrated by those against it.
(*Adapted from Rye, Ison and Santos, 2003*)

Local people

One of the peculiarities of local policy is the role of people, and their relationship with local consultation processes, policy networks, and political campaigns. Local government is the closest form of government to 'the people', and many environmental problems, policy decisions, and policy have an impact at the local level. For example, a decision at the national level to invest in wind farm development will inevitably affect particular areas and communities, as wind farms must be located in an appropriate location with sufficient space and appropriate meteorological conditions. As such, the implementation of national level environmental policies can be fraught with difficulty. While such policies are aimed at solving problems at a national or global level the impacts associated with their development are felt most at the local level. This is also true of local policy decisions, for example, the siting of a waste disposal incinerator, or landfill site. Such policy developments can lead to local opposition which delays the decision-making process.

Local protesters are often described as 'NIMBYs' (not in my back yard). The term NIMBY is used in a wide range of contexts (from the siting of prisons, drug users' rehabilitation centres, nuclear power plants, incinerator plants and wind farms). Of particular interest is the protests surrounding developments that are intended to mitigate environmental problems, rather than those that contribute to them. 'NIMBY' opposition in this context is usually supportive of environmental protection *per se*, but is concerned with the personal cost associated with specific proposals. Concerns about effects on the community including negative impacts on health, environmental quality, and property values, combined with a general decline in confidence in the ability of government and industry to make informed, prudent and equitable decisions about technologies, all contribute towards local opposition. Kraft and Clary (1990, 303) argue that as perceived risk increases, so does opposition to the proposed development. The role played by NIMBYs has been seen as leading to a 'democratic deficit' where a minority prevent policy decisions supported by the majority. For example, NIMBY action can delay developments for long periods of time, and in some cases can make it impossible for them to proceed. Those who condemn NIMBY action argue that it can restrict or delay local economic development and the use of superior technical solutions, and can hamper sustainable development (especially in the case of wind farms). They also label NIMBY action as selfish, irrational and costly to society (Kraft and Clary, 1990). Burningham (2000, 56–7) outlines the three main perspectives on the NIMBY response:

1. NIMBY as an ignorant or irrational response – drawing a clear distinction between the real risks or impacts and the public's assessment of these;
2. NIMBY as a selfish response – protest is not based on wider social/ environmental concerns, but those relating to self-interest such as property value;
3. NIMBY as prudent – public knowledge and concerns are valid, and are rooted in an ability to gather information and evidence that often contradicts that of the experts.

The last provides an interesting contrast to points 1 and 2. Indeed, the public's position on siting issues may be rational and politically legitimate, since citizens may have a fairly good grasp of the issues and a reasonable concern for the genuine risks to community health and welfare that are ignored by technical and administrative elites. Local opposition may serve a broader public interest by identifying important weaknesses in expert analyses about siting and forcing consideration of a broader range of sites (this can provide a way in which citizens can influence policy (Kraft and Clary, 1990, 301) (see Chapter Three). Proponents of this view argue that local consultation and participation about local developments in the first place can use local knowledge and help to allay local concerns. The term NIMBY is also criticised as it is a label carelessly applied to all siting conflicts where strong public opposition is present (Burningham, 2000, 60; Kraft and Clary, 1990, 304).

Participation in decision-making

Local government lends itself to participation, given its proximity to the public. It is an important dimension when it comes to understanding how environmental issues (and solutions) manifest themselves 'on the ground'. Bell et al (2005) suggest that changes to the planning process from confrontation to collaboration might aid the decision-making process, commenting that 'A collaborative approach is grounded in the claim that "deliberative" rather than "technical" rationality should be the basis for environmental decision-making' (Bell et al, 2005, 467).

By involving the local community from the beginning – even before the specific (for example, wind farms and waste incinerators) site is chosen – there may be more incentive for local people to participate (Bell et al, 2005, 468). Deliberative forms of decision-making can also play an educative role, informing both local people about the proposed development, and also decision makers about local concerns.

In general, proponents of participation suggest that it can both improve policy outcomes by drawing on lay knowledge, and can act as an arbitrator between local politicians, policy makers, experts and the public, helping to reduce misunderstandings and conflict that may have arisen as a result of proposed policy changes. Box 5.3 below demonstrates the important role of participation in deer management in Australia. In this instance, wildlife managers conducted numerous forms of consultation and participation with key stakeholders (for example, people living in the most affected areas, wildlife groups and recreational hunting groups) in order to develop the effective management strategies. The project set out to investigate the most effective forms of participation, barriers to participation, and the policy implications of participation.

Box 5.3: Participation case study

Environmental policy can only be truly effective if it addresses both ecological and social goals together. The project 'Conservation, society and invasive species' explored the ways of achieving this in the context of invasive species management in Australia – an economically, environmentally and socially important issue for the country, but also a significant problem globally.

The project first examined the different features of participation in invasive species management programmes across Australia, and how these features relate to achieving ecological and social goals (see Ford-Thompson et al, 2012). One of the participation features explored was the *changes in stakeholder interactions*, which reflects the progression from conflict to cooperation. The study found more improvement in interactions if there were a greater variety of stakeholders involved in the programme, and if the programme was initiated by citizens rather than the government. The study found that conflicts can decrease the participation in programmes, which is problematic if the participants are needed to carry out on-the-ground wildlife management activities, help make decisions, or to provide information or data.

Conflicts between stakeholders can arise from many reasons. Through exploring the social and political context of invasive deer management, the project identified a number of contributing factors, including different political ideologies between government departments and the effect of political history and culture on public attitudes and legislation. The project also developed a framework for understanding and addressing public attitudes, identifying three main dimensions – the stakeholder dimension (concerned with relationships between government and communities, and within communities), the wildlife dimension (concerned with impacts of and perceptions towards invasive species) and the management dimension (concerned with the methods and practicalities of managing invasive species). The framework provides a basis for understanding and responding to the social dimension of wildlife management, facilitating policy makers and managers in achieving both ecological and social goals.

The project was able to make a number of recommendations for improving invasive species management, and the key process underlying these recommendations is stakeholder participation. Although participation cannot resolve all conflicts, if carried out appropriately it can help build social capital, including improving communication and trust, and guiding policy makers on the issues that are important to society.

The project was carried out by researchers at the University of York, and was funded by the Australian Invasive Animals Cooperative Research Centre and the UK Economic and Social Research Council.
(*Case study written by Adriana Ford-Thompson*)

Encouraging individual behavioural change

The global nature of environmental issues has resulted in a progressive shift towards to governing environmental issues at the regional and local level (Barr et al, 2011). This has resulted environmental policy increasingly influencing the behaviour and resource consumption of organisation, individuals and communities (Owens, 2000). For example, many activities that contribute to greenhouse gas emissions and resource use result from the choices made by individuals, households, businesses and other stakeholders at the local community level. If national target greenhouse gas emissions reductions targets are to be met then individuals and communities will need to change the way they consume and produce goods and services (Mulugetta et al, 2010). This is a challenge as many sections of the community have still yet to be convinced by the need to change. Additional effort is therefore required to promote sustainable lifestyles and foster pro-environmental behavioural change at the community level (Heiskanen et al, 2010).

The lifestyles we lead are the different personal actions that allow us to differentiate ourselves from others in society (Campbell, 1998; Chaney, 1996). The largest environmental impacts of day-to-day personal actions are associated with housing, food, energy and personal travel (Gronco and Warde, 2001; Lorek and Spangenberg, 2001; Spangenberg and Lorek, 2002). What constitutes a sustainable or 'green' lifestyle is closely linked to the political discourse of sustainability, which may change over time. A sustainable lifestyle can be seen as one that minimises the use of natural resources, waste and polluting emissions and does not jeopardise the needs of future generations (Bedford et al, 2004). Considerable guidance exists on how to reduce the impact of consumption and lead a green lifestyle. Such guidance outlines a range of different actions promoted in national and local government campaigns to reduce an individual's environmental impact (see Table 5.2 and also Chapter Four).

Understanding the factors that influence how and why decisions are made and the willingness and potential to change consumption choices is critical to achieving long-term attitudinal and behavioural change (Bedford et al, 2004; Jackson, 2005). These factors include knowledge (for example, how individuals interpret information based on existing beliefs), psychological factors (for example, values, attitudes and emotions that affect behaviour and give a sense of responsibility), habits (for example, behaviour that contributes to greenhouse gas emissions is often habitual and routine), structural conditions (for example, infrastructure – or lack of – can lead to 'lock-in' situations providing an obstacle to behavioural change) and socio-demographic patterns (for example, the influence of these factors vary with individual circumstances) (Haq et al, 2008; Sanne, 2002).

Approaches to achieving pro-environmental behavioural change include top-down mass information and awareness campaigns directed at the whole population (see Table 5.3), such as the UK government's energy saving/environmental campaigns: 'Save It' (mid-1970s), 'Are You Doing Your Bit?' (late 1990s) and 'Act on CO_2' (2007) (Hinchliffe, 1996; Owens, 2000). These campaigns are based on a rationalist information deficit model and aim to 'educate' the public by providing information to allow rational decisions and behaviours. However, such campaigns tend to be intensive, limited in time and expensive. The top-down approach has been criticised for misunderstanding public perceptions of a particular issue (Owens, 2000, see also Chapter Three). Factors that might influence or have an impact on a decision are often ignored, such as: people's perception of sustainable goods and services as being more expensive; lack of awareness about how to become more sustainable; and mistrust of government bodies and businesses that promote lifestyle changes (Holdsworth and Steedman, 2005).

In contrast, social marketing techniques and the development of personalised and collective community-based approaches have also

Table 5.2: Actions that constitute a 'Green' lifestyle

Energy	Food and products	Transport	Water	Waste
Switch from electric to gas cookers and condensing boilers	Reduce meat and dairy consumption	Modal shift to reduce air travel	Fit a toilet water-saving device	Recycle household waste
Insulate homes and fit double glazing	Reduce fish consumption purchase fish from sustainable stocks	Modal shift from cars to public transport	Install low-flow taps and showers	Dispose of toxic materials safety
Reduce temperature of the home environment	Purchase locally grown produce	Walking and cycling short distances	Reduce use of water (for example, car, washing, lawn and sprinklers and dish washers)	Compost organic waste
Purchase energy-efficient appliances and do not leave appliances in standby mode	Reduce levels of highly processed foods	Using smaller fuel-efficient cars and car share		
Reduce temperature of wash cycles to 40°C	Purchase certified sustainable wood and paper products			
	Live in multiple person households			

Source: Based on Bedford et al, 2004

Table 5.3: Approaches to achieving pro-environmental behavioural change

	Top-down social campaigns	Personalized social marketing	Community-based social marketing
Focus	Individual	Individual	Community/ Individual
Example	National energy conservation campaigns to save energy	SmartTravel campaigns to reduce car use	Eco-Teams to reduce community/ household environmental footprint
Steps			
1	Information	Direct contact	Concern
2	Knowledge	Motivation	Collective motivation
3	Attitude	Information/ Knowledge	Information/ Knowledge
4	Value	Experimentation	Experimentation
5	Behavioural change	Behavioural change	Behavioural change

Source: Based on Brög, et al, 2002

addressed the issue of voluntary behavioural change. These have been successful in fostering specific behaviour changes related to public health such as smoking, alcohol consumption and exercise (Turning Point, 2003). Social marketing has been defined as 'the use of marketing principles and techniques to influence a target audience to voluntarily accept, reject, modify or abandon behavior for the benefit of individuals, groups or society as a whole' (Kotler and Roberto, 1989). Social marketing combines knowledge from psychology and marketing with audience segmentation being a key component (Geller, 1989). Segmentation involves understanding and identifying the individuals that make up a particular target group and developing appropriate and tailor-made communication messages, information and incentives. Social marketing also uses socio-psychological tools to motivate change, such as 'prompts', which are visual or audio-aids designed to remind people to behave in certain ways. It also provides incentives to motivate people to engage in different actions (Kassirer and McKenzie-Mohr,

1998; McKenzie-Mohr and Smith, 1999; McKenzie-Mohr, 2000; Haq et al, 2008).

However, social marketing approaches tend to empower the individual to make an informed and conscious choice, which to some extent is self-reinforcing (McClaren, 1998). Implicit in social marketing is that behavioural change can only emerge within existing dominant discourses of consumptions especially in the 'home'. Social marketing initiatives have been used to foster pro-environmental behavioural change and the adoption of low carbon lifestyle changes with regard to energy, waste and recycling (Hobson, 2003; Staats and Harland, 1995) and travel (for example, personalised travel planning) (Australian Greenhouse Office, 2006; Haq et al, 2008). These have been aimed at the individual, household and community level and have been popular with the UK Department for Food, Environment and Rural Affairs (Defra) which has embraced the notion of citizen-consumers and have adopted a social marketing approach to sustainable lifestyles.

Social marketing has been criticised for being unambitious, focusing on marginal small-scale actions which are considered insufficient to address the magnitude of the environmental challenges that lie ahead (Peattie and Peattie, 2009). A number of key limitations of social marketing have been identified (Corner and Randall, 2011). These include the focus on differences between individuals using segmentation and tailoring messages to individual beliefs, values and preferences which could make greener behaviour less likely to be sustained over time. For example, people who hold strong self-enhancing materialistic values are less likely to engage in greener behaviour for collective well-being (Kasser et al, 2007). Social marketing initiatives could also inhabit the potential of social networks to influence behaviour as they focus on the individual and therefore and run the risks of exacerbating differences (Haythornthwaite, 1996; Fell et al, 2009). There is also little evidence to suggest that social marketing initiatives aimed at affecting one lifestyle choices in the home necessarily leads to positive behaviour changes in other areas such as work (that is, 'spillover effect') and in some cases can be negative by where the reverse effect is observed (Thøgersen,1999; Thøgersen and Ölander,

2002, 2003; Crompton and Thorgersen, 2009). Social and spatial context in which individual behaviours are performed is also considered important (Barr et al, 2011). While individuals are committed to greener behaviour in and around the home they may be unwilling to reduce carbon intensive activities such as flying. Therefore differences exist between a household and touristic context. For example, when on holiday consumption is not challenged. This has the potential to result in an inversion in behaviours between home and the holiday location. Social marketing therefore needs to be adapted to address more carbon intensive activities as small scale change is still perceived as not being enough.

Involve/DEA (2010) examined three broad approaches to influencing pro-environmental behavioural change: 'nudge' based on Thaler and Susntein's (2008) 'nudge theory'; 'think' using deliberative engagement (for example, information and education) and 'shove' using legal compulsion and penalty to restrict behaviour and choice. Thaler and Susntein's (2008) 'nudge' theory' suggests that positive reinforcement and/or suggestion can influence the motives, drivers and decision-making of groups and individuals. 'Nudge' does not seek to engage or influence people's values and attitudes but can be just as efficient if not more than direct instruction, legislation or enforcement. The UK government's Behavioural Insights Team was set up in 2010 to finds ways to encourage, support and enable people to make better choices for themselves and strongly influenced by 'nudge' theory. It has covered a number of these including public health, consumer empowerment and growth, energy efficiency and climate change. Involve/DEA (2010) argue that these different approaches depend on each other for their effectiveness and an optimal mix should be used to transform social values and attitudes.

While regulation and enforcement are key elements in achieving improved environmental quality, the 'ABC' (attitude → behaviour → choice) model of behavioural change, has not necessarily achieved the fundamental shift required in consumption patterns (see Chapter Three). Structural and psychological issues can limit and influence individual consumer choice and behaviour. Unlike a change in awareness that often erodes over time or does not convert to actual behavioural change, voluntary behavioural change, especially as demonstrated with social marketing can achieve behavioural change. Individuals are more likely to engage in greener behaviour if they perceive that the motivation comes from within rather than from an external controlling agent. People act because the behaviour is enjoyable, challenging or because they endorse the values underlying the action (Osbaldiston and Sheldon, 2003). Voluntary approaches allow the individual to acquire new skills as a result of an empowerment process that is consistently reinforced by personal benefits gained (for example, improved health, more free time, reduced stress, reduced cost, etc) (Marinelli and Roth, 2002). The focus on voluntary 'simple and painless' behavioural changes are seen as having the potential to lead to greater public acceptance of government interventions. However, they could reinforce the perception that environmental challenges can be adequately met through simple voluntary actions and suggestions for more ambitious government intervention are disproportionate and unnecessary (Crompton and Thorgersen, 2009).

If voluntary pro-environmental behaviour are to be effective they will need to outline simple steps in the context of a broader social engagement that address the fundamental aspects of the environmental challenge including ensuring that government and industry play their part in environmental protection. Such initiatives will need to be implemented within a supportive institutional/social, infrastructural and fiscal framework that reinforces and fosters greener behaviour.

SUMMARY

- Approaches to sustainable development have largely focused on 'weak' understandings of the concept, and may limit the effectiveness of resulting policies.
- A lack of full scientific evidence, the misinterpretation or misuse (either deliberately or otherwise) of evidence, and politicisation of science may undermine the case for action.
- Some characterise the international policy arena as one of anarchy, given the lack of international government.
- At the national level, supranational organisations such as the EU may affect policy direction and progress.
- At the national level there are a number of theories that may help explain policy change: policy network analysis helps us to consider the role of those involved in the decision-making process, whereas theories of incrementalism and path dependency help to explain policy stability. Punctuated equilibrium may help inform understandings of policy change.
- At the local level the makeup and role of local government, policy networks, and local politics are all said to influence policy.
- Many conflicts over environmental policies are played out at the local level, with the term NIMBY sometimes used to describe those protesting against developments such as wind farms or recycling plants.
- Environmental policy is increasingly influencing the behaviour and resource consumption of organisation, individuals and communities.
- Many sections of the community have still yet to be convinced by the need to change their behaviour.
- Approaches to achieving pro-environmental behavioural change include top-down mass information and awareness campaigns directed at the whole population as well as personalised social marketing and collective community-based approaches

READING GUIDE

Baker, S, 2006, *Sustainable development*, London: Routledge

Carter, N, 2007, *The politics of the environment*, 2nd edn, Cambridge: Cambridge University Press

Chasek, P, Downie, D, Brown, J, 2006, *Global environmental politics*, 4th edn, Boulder, CO: Westview Press

Crompton, T, Thøgersen, J, 2009, *Simple and painless? The limitations of spillover in environmental campaigning*, Godalming: Worldwide Fund for Nature

Devine-Wright, P, 2011, *Renewable energy and the public: From NIMBY to participation*, London: Earthscan

Hill, M, 2009, The Policy Process, 5th edn, Harlow: Pearson

Hulme, M, 2009, *Why we disagree about climate change*, Cambridge: Cambridge University Press

Luke, WT, 2005, Neither sustainable nor development: Reconsidering sustainability in development, *Sustainable Development* 13, 228–38

Moser, S, Bovkoff, M, 2013, *Successful adaptation to climate change: Linking science and policy in a rapidly changing world*, Abingdon: Routledge

Oreskes, N, 2004, Science and public policy: What's proof got to do with it?, *Environmental Science and Policy* 7, 369–83

Thaler, RH, Susntein, CR, 2008, *Nudge: Improving decisions about health, wealth and happiness*, New Haven, CT: Yale University Press

6

Future environmental challenges

Introduction

Despite improvements in environmental quality over the last four decades many regions of the world are still seriously affected by major environmental problems. Current and future environmental challenges include climate change, urban air pollution, deforestation, land degradation, marine pollution, loss of biodiversity, waste and chemical pollution, food, water and energy insecurity (UNEP, 2012). The extent to which a particular country or region is affected by an environmental challenge will be dependent on their vulnerability and capacity to adapt to future environmental change. For example in Africa, Asia, the Pacific, Latin America and the Caribbean common challenges include population growth, increasing consumption, rapid urbanisation placing increasing stress on diminishing natural resources. Europe and North America continue to operate at unsustainable levels of consumption, and North America in particular has seen limited growth in the renewable energy industry. West Asia is facing worsening water scarcity, land degradation and sea level rise (UNEP, 2012).

This chapter examines the major drivers that contribute to environmental change which have exceeded natural ecological limits, in particular, the pressure placed on food, water and energy security. It discusses the role of new governance structures, green economy, political will and public acceptance in addressing future environmental challenges.

Tectonic shifts affecting environmental change

As assessment of global future trends suggests that there will be a number of international tectonic shifts. These major social, economic and environmental shifts will be critical to the global environment and will determine the way the world will operate in the future (NIC, 2012). Table 6.1 presents the key tectonic shifts that are likely to affect environmental change up to 2030. These global drivers include population growth and economic development that can exert particular pressure on the environment via transport, urbanisation and globalisation (UNEP, 2012). Environmental pressures can result in a change in the state of the environment and cause a wide range of socio-economic and environmental impacts. Rising public and political concern over these impacts can lead to greater environmental regulation (Smeets and Weterings, 1999; Tscherning et al, 2011).

Current forecasts suggest that the global population will reach 10 billion by 2100. A larger and richer population increases demand on natural systems for resources such as food, water and energy. As discussed in Chapter Two, it also can also cause environmental pollution due to greater urbanisation and land use change. A major part of this growth will take place in developing countries whose population is projected to rise to 6 billion by 2050 and 9 billion by 2100. While the population is growing it is also ageing, with the number of people aged 60 and over expected to reach 2 billion in 2050 and 3 billion in 2100. This could increase the number of people vulnerable to the impact of future environmental change (see Box 6.1) (UNPD, 2010).

Currently, over half of the world's population lives in urban centres. By 2050 6.3 billion people will be residing in cities. Nearly all of the expected growth in the world population will be concentrated in the urban areas of the less developed regions, whose population is projected to reach 5.1 billion in 2050. In the more developed regions, the urban population is projected to increase modestly, from 1 billion in 2011 to 1.1 billion in 2050 (UNDESA, 2011).

Table 6.1: Tectonic shifts affecting environmental change by 2030

Growth of the global middle class	Middle classes most everywhere in the developing world are poised to expand substantially in terms of both absolute numbers and the percentage of the population that can claim middle-class status during the next 15–20 years.
Wider access to lethal and disruptive technologies	A wider spectrum of instruments of war – especially precision-strike capabilities, cyber instruments, bioterror weaponry – will become accessible. Individuals and small groups will have the capability to penetrate large-scale and disruption – a capability formerly the monopoly of states.
Definitive shift of economic power to the East and South	The US, European, and Japanese share of global income is projected to fall from 56 per cent today to under half by 2030. In 2008, China overtook the US as the world's largest saver, by 2020, emerging markets' share of financial assets is project to almost double.
Unprecedented and widespread ageing	Whereas in 2012 only Japan and Germany have matured by a median age of 45, most European countries, South Korea, and Taiwan will have entered the post-mature age category by 2030. Migration will become more globalised as both rich and developing countries suffer from work force shortages.
Urbanisation	The current urban population will increase from approximately 50 to 60 per cent or 4.9 billion people by 2030. Africa will gradually replace Asia as the region with the highest urbanisation growth rate. Urban centres are estimated to generate 80 per cent of economic growth; the potential exists to apply modern technologies and infrastructure, promoting better use of scarce resources.
Food and water pressures	Demand for food is expected to rise at least 35 per cent by 2030 while demand for water is expected to rise by 40 per cent. Nearly half of the world's population will live in areas experiencing food and water shortages, but China and India are also vulnerable.

Source: NIC, 2012

Box 6.1: Global ageing and environmental change

By 2050 there will be an unprecedented increase in the number of people aged 55-plus, representing nearly a quarter of the global population. The interaction between an ageing population and the environment poses significant challenges and opportunities for public policy.

Older people are a diverse group and some are physically, financially and emotionally less resilient in coping with the effects of environmental change than others. The insecurity and heightened exposure to environmental threats are compounded for some older people by their reduced capacity for coping independently in later life. A subset of older people can be disproportionately affected by natural disasters, climate-related weather events and levels of pollution, especially in the developing world where basic health and social care is often absent.

Growing old in the twenty-first century will bring with it the unique challenge of a changing global environment with variable climate and weather patterns which will have an impact on all aspects of life. In order to effectively manage the impacts associated with environmental change, it will be necessary to confront and integrate social dimensions in adaptation planning. This requires a better understanding of the effects a changing environment will have on older people at the local, regional, national and international level and in different geographical and socio-economic contexts.

(Haq et al, 2013)

Population, income, production and consumption of products and services are the key drivers that have resulted in a wide range of environmental problems. Globalisation has improved the living standards of many people but has also increased the global competition for scarce land, water, energy and natural assets. Global material extraction has been estimated to range from 47 to 59 billion tonnes per year at the turn of the twenty-first century and is growing rapidly. The extraction of resources, processing of raw materials and the production of polluting emissions and waste all have an impact on the environment (Steinberger et al, 2010). Primary industries such as mining and forestry use raw natural resources, which ultimately results in products that are bought and used and discarded by individual consumers. As demand for natural resources increases there will be intense strategic resource competition between nation states that could eventually lead to increased poverty, state fragility, inflation and economic instability (Evans, 2010).

The impact of population growth and economic development must be set alongside the impact of per capita consumption. For example, if everyone lived like an average resident of the USA, a total of four Earths would be required to regenerate humanity's annual demand on nature. In contrast, if all of humanity lived like an average resident of Indonesia, only two-thirds of the planet's biocapacity would be used (WWF, 2012). The rise in global consumption is partly due to the surge in the number of people, especially in the developing world. The increase in consumption threatens offsetting any savings gained in improved resource efficiency. For example, if an average resident of the USA ate 20 per cent less meat in 2050 than in 2000; total US meat consumption will be 5 million tons greater in 2050 due to population growth (WWI, 2013).

Until recently, global consumer demand has been concentrated in the rich developed countries. However, the number of middle-income consumers is growing. Global middle class have been defined as those living in households with daily per capita incomes of between US$10 and US$100 in purchasing power parity per capita terms (Kharas, 2010). It has been estimated that more than half the world's middle class could reside in Asia. With Asian consumers estimated to account for more than 40 per cent of global middle-class consumption. This is due to a large number of Asian households having incomes today that position them just below the global middle class.

As the consumer class thrived the gap between the global rich and poor has widened. Approximately 60 per cent of private consumption spending is undertaken by 12 per cent of the world's population who live in North American and Western Europe. This is in contrast to one-third of consumers living in South Asia and Sub-Saharan Africa who account for only 3.2 per cent of private consumption spending (WWI, 2013).

Population growth, economic development and rising consumption are among the many factors that have contributed to increasing human pressure on the global environment that has now exceeded natural ecological limits.

Human footprint and planetary boundaries

Since the 1970s, humanity's ecological footprint has doubled (see Box 6.2). In 2008 the footprint exceeded the Earth's biocapacity (the area actually available to produce renewable resources and absorb carbon dioxide) by more than 50 per cent. It would take 1.5 years for the Earth to produce the resources humanity consumes in a single year (see Figure 6.1). This 'ecological overshoot' is largely attributable to the carbon footprint, which has increased eleven-fold since 1961. Carbon emissions in particular together with food demand, are the major drivers of the escalating footprint (WWF, 2012).

Box 6.2: Ecological footprint

The ecological footprint tracks humanity's demands on the biosphere by comparing the renewable resources people are consuming against the Earth's regenerative capacity, or biocapacity: the area of land actually available to produce renewable resources and absorb carbon dioxide emissions. Both the ecological footprint and biocapacity are expressed in a common unit called a global hectare, in which one global hectare represents a biologically productive hectare with world average productivity (WWF, 2012).

Figure 6.1: Global ecological footprint

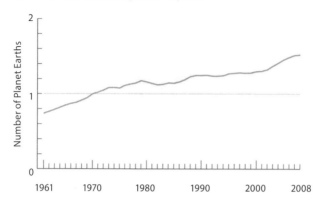

Source: WWF, 2012

Humanity's footprint is placing increasing pressure on the Earth's ecosystem which is now believed to have reached a point where rapid global environmental change is possible (Rockström et al, 2011). A total of nine planetary boundaries have been identified: climate change, stratospheric ozone, land use change, freshwater use, biological diversity, ocean acidification, nitrogen and phosphorus inputs to the biosphere and oceans, aerosol loading and chemical pollution (see Figure 6.2). Three of these planetary boundaries have already been transgressed: climate change, biological diversity and nitrogen input to the biosphere (see Table 6.2). Since the boundaries are strongly connected crossing one boundary may seriously threaten the ability to stay within safe levels of the others. The extent to which human societies will be affected by transgressing these planetary boundaries will be dependent on their ability to cope with rapid environmental change. As described throughout this short guide, it is often the poorest communities with weak infrastructures and social support services which are most at risk.

Figure 6.2: Beyond planetary boundaries

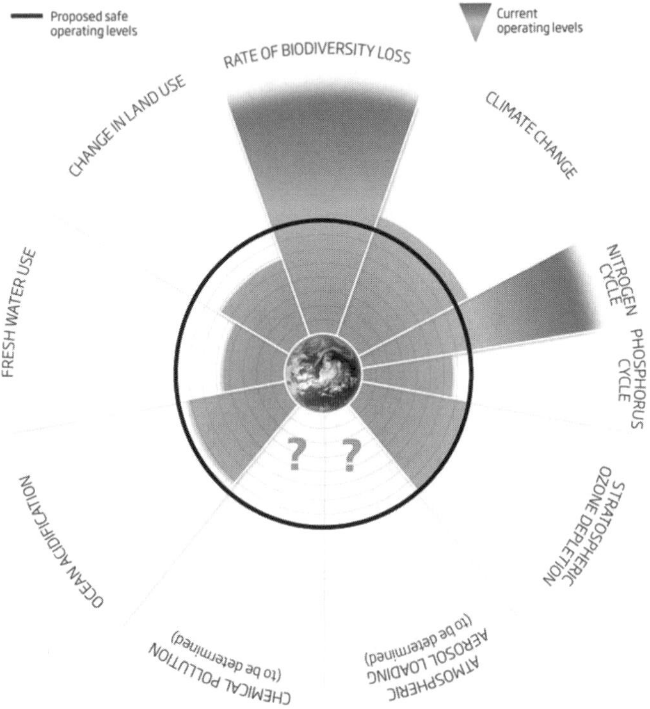

Source: Rockström et al, 2011

The increasing interconnection between food, water and energy in combination with climate change will have far-reaching effects on global development. An increasing population, urbanisation, motorisation, expanding middle class, income distribution and changes in consumption patterns will all increase the demand for critical natural resources such as food, water and energy. The scale and pace to meet the demand for resources will be further affected by environmental issues such as biodiversity loss, deforestation, soil erosion and land degradation, water and air pollution (Chatham House, 2012). This could result in the insecurity and availability of certain resources due to their scarcity (Keys and Malnight, 2012). The availability and price of one resource will have knock-on effects in the production of other

Table 6.2: Planetary boundaries

Earth-system process	Parameters	Proposed boundary	Current status	Pre-industrial value
Climate change	Atmospheric carbon dioxide (parts per million by volume)	350	387	280
	Change in radiative forcing (watts per metre squared)	1	1.5	0
Rate of biodiversity loss	Extinction rate (number of species per million per year)	10	>100	0.1–1
Nitrogen cycle (part of a boundary with the phosphorus cycle)	Amount of nitrogen removed from the atmosphere for human use (millions of tonnes per year)	35	121	0
Phosphorus cycle (part of a boundary with the nitrogen cycle)	Quantity of phosphorus flowing in the oceans (millions of tonnes per year)	11	8.5–9.5	-1
Stratospheric ozone depletion	Concentration of ozone (Dobson unit)	276	283	290
Ocean acidification	Global mean saturation state of aragonite in surface sea water	2.75	2.90	3.44
Global freshwater use	Consumption of freshwater by humans (km^3 per year)	4,000	2,600	415
Change in land use	Percentage of global land cover converted to cropland	15	11.7	Low
Atmospheric aerosol	Overall particulate concentration in atmosphere, on a regional basis	To be determined		
Chemical pollution	For example, emitted to or concentration of persistent organic compounds, plastics, endocrine disrupters, heavy metals and nuclear waste in the global environment, or the effects of ecosystems of the function of Earth system.	To be determined		

Source: Rockström et al, 2011

resources (Chatham House, 2012). Changes in patterns of production, trade and use of natural resources are expected to reshape national and international politics and relationships. Table 6.3 provides an overview of the future of natural resources and shows that long-term forecasts predict a high demand growth for most natural resources until at least 2030.

Table 6.3: Future outlook for natural resources

	By 2020	By 2030
Food	Average crops prices increase by 15–20% against long-rate average, but lower than 2008–10 spike	Cereal prices increase by 70–90% compared with 2010; up to 130–170% with climate change
	Global food production grows by 1.5% per year	Crop demand reaches 2.7 billion tonnes, from 1.9 billion tonnes in the 1990s
	Stocks-to-use ratios remain at crisis thresholds	Meat demand growth between 2001 and 2030 estimated at 1.7% per year
	Fish-as-food demand increases by 11–17% compared to 2010	Fish-as-food demand grows by 20–30% compared with 2010
Energy	Demand for energy increases by 17% (from 2010) by 2020	Demand for energy grows by 29%. Coal demand grows by 20% and gas by 44%.
	To meet oil supply in 2020, over US $3 trillion of investment in the oil sector is needed.	By 2035 a total of US$37 trillion investments is needed in the energy sector, half of which will go to the power sector.
	Prices for oil are around US$120 barrel. Gas prices remains differentiated by regions, with Asia being significantly higher than North America's	Prices for oil are at US$100–140 per barrel in real terms
Metals	30–50% demand growth for major metals; rare earth demand doubles from 2010 levels	90% demand growth for steel, 60% for copper (2020 baseline). Demand for aluminium more than doubles.
	Copper faces a 30% supply gap in absence of considerable additional investment	Copper could face a 50% supply gap in absence of considerable additional investment.
	Heavy rare earths remain in deficit until 2018–20	Potential for temporary shortages of speciality metals with wider deployment of novel technologies

Source: Chatham House, 2012

Food, water and energy nexus

Climate change

Climate change has led to changes in climate extremes such as heat waves, record high temperatures and, in many regions, heavy precipitation in the past half century (IPCC, 2012b). Climate extremes or even a series of non-extreme events, in combination with social vulnerabilities and exposure to risks are expected to result in climate-related disasters. An IPCC (2012b) Special Report on *Managing the risks of extreme events and disasters to advance climate change adaptation* concluded that:

- It is likely (66–100 per cent probability) that the frequency of heavy precipitation will increase in the twenty-first century over many regions.
- It is virtually certain (99–100 per cent probability) that increases in the frequency of warm daily temperature extremes and decreases in cold extremes will occur throughout the twenty-first century on a global scale.
- It is very likely (90–100 per cent probability) that heat waves will increase in length, frequency, and/or intensity over most land areas.
- It is likely (66–100 per cent probability) that the average maximum wind speed of tropical cyclones (also known as typhoons or hurricanes) will increase throughout the coming century, although possibly not in every ocean basin.
- It is also likely (66–100 per cent probability) that overall there will be either a decrease or essentially no change in the number of tropical cyclones.

Water, agriculture and food, health and tourism sectors are expected to be more affected by extreme weather events. As described in Chapter Two, regions with basic agricultural practices are more vulnerable to increasing variability in seasonal rainfall, drought and weather extremes. Vulnerability is further exacerbated by population growth, degradation of ecosystems and overuse of natural resources, as well as poor standards for health, education and governance (IPCCC, 2012b).

Climate change will have different regional impacts on food and water security. The IPCCC provide medium confidence that droughts will intensify over the coming century in southern Europe and the Mediterranean region, central Europe, central North America, Central America and Mexico, northeast Brazil and southern Africa. It is very likely that average sea level rise will contribute to upward trends in extreme sea levels in extreme coastal high water levels. Projected precipitation and temperature changes imply changes in floods, although overall there is low confidence at the global scale regarding climate-driven changes in the magnitude or frequency of river-related flooding due to limited evidence (IPCCC, 2012b).

Food

There is increasing concern about food security and the ability of the world to provide a healthy and environmentally sustainable diet for all. Agricultural output will need to increase by at least 60 per cent in the next decades if the planet is to feed a growing population that is expected to reach 9 billion people in 2050 (FAO, 2012b). Nearly 1 billion people currently suffer from hunger and do not eat enough calories or consume enough protein, vitamins or minerals (Godfray et al, 2010). Climate change will make it even harder to feed a growing population as it reduces the productivity of the majority of existing food systems and affects the livelihoods of those who are already vulnerable to food insecurity (CFS, 2012).

Water

Water is a key requirement for food and energy. It is required for the production of crops and livestock that are highly water-intensive. Water is also used in the production of all sources of energy and electricity, that is, the extraction of raw materials, cooling in thermal processes, cleaning processes, culture of crops for biofuels, and powering turbines (UNESCO and WWAP, 2012). Agriculture accounts for 70 per cent of all water withdrawn by the agriculture, municipal and industrial (including energy) sectors combined (UNESCO and WWAP, 2012). The high demand for livestock products increases the demand for water. This affects water quality which in turn reduces availability. There is high uncertainty with the prediction of future demand for water in agricultural. Future global water consumption (including rain fed and irrigated agriculture) are expected to increase by approximately 19 per cent by 2050. However, much of this increase in water consumption will be in water-scarce regions (UNESCO and WWAP, 2012).

Energy

Global energy consumption is expected to increase by 36 per cent in the period 2011–30. This will be mainly in the power generation (49 per cent) and industry (31 per cent) sectors. Almost all this growth in energy demand (93 per cent) will be from emerging economies. China and India account for more than half of this increase in energy demand (BP, 2013).

Although the fuel mix is evolving, fossil fuels continue to dominate. By 2030 oil, gas and coal are expected to have market shares of approximately 26–28 per cent compared to non-fossil fuels which are expected to have a share of approximately 6–7 per cent each (nuclear, hydro and renewables). Unconventional energy sources (for example, shale gas, biofuels and tight oil) are playing an increasing role in transforming the energy balance. For example, it is predicted that by 2030 the USA will be 99 per cent self-sufficient in net energy (BP, 2013). This will be due to increasing production of unconventional energy sources and moderating energy demand. In contrast, major emerging economies such as China and India that are experiencing rapid economic growth are becoming increasingly reliant on energy imports.

Demand for natural gas is expected to increase on average by 2 per cent per year up to 2030 with 76 per cent of this demand coming from emerging economies. By 2030 shale gas supplies are expected to meet 37 per cent of the growth in gas demand and account for 16 per cent of world gas and 53 per cent of US gas production by 2030 (BP, 2013).

Shale gas has been controversial due to the environmental impact of the 'fracking' process used to extract the gas (see Box 6.3).

Box 6.3: Fracking

Shale gas is obtained in a process called hydraulic fracturing or 'fracking' and can use hydraulic drilling. The process is considered controversial with concern over land and water use, net effects on greenhouse gas emissions, risk of groundwater contamination and potential seismic activity (House of Commons Library, 2012). Fracking involves drilling a hole deep into the shale rocks that contain natural gas. A large quantity of water mixed with sand and chemicals is then pumped into the rock. This creates tiny fissures in the rock which allow the trapped gas to escape and be captured and piped off. Approximately a third of the waste water, which contains treatments, sands and other chemicals is returned to the surface. Since many shale deposits are buried under aquifers there has been growing concern that the process of drilling and fracking could release chemicals into the aquifer as well as methane leaks which can cause fires and explosions.

Safe shale gas could boost energy diversity and security if undertaken in an environmentally acceptable manner. The International Energy Agency has developed a set of 'golden rules' for shale gas extraction which is estimated to increase the cost of developing a shale gas well site by 7 per cent. IEA believe that following such guidelines would increase industry, public and environmental acceptance of shale gas extraction (IEA, 2012a).

By 2030 renewable energy's (for example, solar, wind, hydro) share of global electricity production is expected to grow from 4 per cent in 2011 to 11 per cent by 2030. Non-OECD economies are expected to account for 41 per cent of the total by 2030.

Carbon emissions from energy use are expected to increase by 26 per cent between 2011 and 2030, with emissions higher than that required to stabilise the concentration of greenhouse gas emissions at the recommended level of 450 ppm. Energy-related carbon emissions in the EU, US and China are expected to fall due to a number of factors such as abatement policies, expansion of renewables, increased energy efficiency and structural change.

Meeting the environmental challenge

Environmental challenges are becoming increasingly multi-dimensional with wider-ranging social and economic impacts and a higher degree of uncertainty. A more balanced approach to environmental, economic and social concerns needs to be adopted to address these challenges. This will require new governance structures, transformative policies and innovative technologies to overcome barriers to sustainable development (UNEP, 2012). Individuals, institutions and countries and the global community have a key role to play in responding to environmental challenges. This will require enhancing and building capacity to address environmental issues especially in the developing world, providing more reliable data for informed environmental policy making and public awareness, developing and adopting new innovative technologies. Traditionally environmental groups have opposed the use of technology such as nuclear power. The use of technology is seen, however, by some as the only way to address global environmental challenges such as climate change (Brand, 2009; Lynas, 2011), with densely populated cities, nuclear energy, GM food, planet-wide geo-engineering to manipulate the Earth's climate to counteract global warming being some of the possible solutions advocated (Brand, 2009).

Environmental concern has caused OECD countries to increase their financial commitment to addressing environmental issues. Aid commitments to three UN conventions of biodiversity, climate change and desertification rose from US$5.1 billion to US$17.4 billion in 1999. In 2010 the same countries allocated US$22.9 billion to development assistance for climate change and adaptation. However, the cost of developing countries to adapt to climate change alone is estimated to be US$70–100 billion a year for the period 2010–50 (UNEP, 2012). Many OECD countries are now coming under increasing pressure to reduce national debt, putting their contribution to international aid at risk.

While there has been international efforts to address environmental problems, progress has been slow. An UN assessment of global environmental goals found that significant progress had only been achieved for four out of the 90 most-important environmental goals (UNEP, 2012). These four goals were: eliminating the production and use of substances that deplete the ozone layer, removal of lead from motor vehicle fuel, increasing access to improved water supplies and boosting research to reduce pollution of the marine environment. Some progress was shown in 40 goals, including the expansion of protected areas such as National Parks and efforts to reduce deforestation. However, little or no progress was detected for 24 environmental goals – including climate change, fish stocks and desertification and drought. Further deterioration was highlighted for eight environmental goals including the state of the world's coral reefs while no assessment was made of 14 other goals due to a lack of data.

Meeting future environmental challenges will require more flexible and adaptive global and national governance frameworks (Dietz et al, 2003). These frameworks will need to be based on clear and measurable goals, verifiable strategies and strong monitoring and evaluation mechanisms (UNEP, 2012). Into order to attain more effective, efficient and equitable outcomes a polycentric governance approach has been advocated (UNEP, 2012). Polycentric governance recognises the diversity of different contexts and assumes multiple centres of activity and authority (Folke et al, 2005). Such an approach meets different capacity needs and provides appropriate responses to environmental challenges. In addition, a systematic and comprehensive results-based global approach could be taken to enhance human wellbeing and environmental sustainability. These could be anchored in six response options to environmental challenges (UNEP, 2012):

- framing environmental goals in the context of sustainable development;
- enhancing the effectiveness of global institutions;
- investing in enhanced capacities for addressing environmental change;
- supporting technological innovation and development;
- strengthening rights-based approaches and access to environmental justice; and
- deepening and broadening stakeholder engagement.

In addition to flexible governance structures, a co-benefits approach needs to be adopted simultaneously to meet different environmental objectives. This is particularly the case in the area of climate policy (see Box 6.4). Developing countries tend to be more concerned with achieving their own development goals than mitigating greenhouse gases (see Chapter Four). Yet some climate actions can mitigate greenhouse gases and local air pollution. Policies aimed at mitigating one of these environmental problems potentially have large effects on the other. For example, climate policy may reduce the demand for coal in the electricity sector, which lowers emissions that contribute to local air pollution (NEAA, 2009).

Box 6.4: Co-benefits of black carbon and tropospheric ozone reduction

A UNEP/WMO (2011) report on *Integrated assessment of black carbon and tropospheric ozone* highlights how a small number of emission reduction measures targeting black carbon and ozone precursors could immediately begin to protect climate, public health, water and food security and ecosystems.

Black carbon exists as particles in the atmosphere and is a major component of soot. At ground level, ozone is an air pollutant harmful to human health and ecosystems and, throughout the lower atmosphere, is also a significant greenhouse gas.

Ozone is not directly emitted, but is produced from emissions of precursors of which methane and carbon monoxide are of particular interest.

Climate benefits from cutting ozone are achieved by reducing emissions of some of its precursors, especially methane which is also a powerful greenhouse gas. These short-lived climate gases (for example, black carbon and methane) only remain in the atmosphere for a short time compared to longer-lived greenhouse gases (for example, carbon dioxide).

Measures advocated include the recovery of methane from coal, oil and gas extraction and transport, methane capture in waste management, use of clean-burning stoves for residential cooking, diesel particulate filters for vehicles and the banning of open burning of agricultural waste.

The study claims that the full implementation of the identified measures would reduce future global warming by 0.5° Celsius (within a range of 0.2°C to 0.7°C). If the measures were to be implemented by 2030, this could halve the potential increase in global temperature projected for 2050 compared to a reference scenario based on current policies and energy and fuel projections. The rate of regional temperature increase would also be reduced.

In addition, implementation of all the measures could avoid 2.4 million premature deaths (within a range of 0.7 to 4.6 million) and the loss of 52 million tonnes (within a range of 30 to 140 million tonnes), 1.4 per cent, of global production of maize, rice, soybean and wheat each year. The most substantial benefits will be felt immediately in or close to the regions where action is taken to reduce emissions, with the greatest health and crop benefits expected.

Green economy

A central issue to address future environmental challenges will be how human wellbeing can be improved and maintained within ecological limits and planetary boundaries. This will require defining wealth and prosperity that goes beyond GDP to an indicator that promotes quality of life and community wellbeing especially in the developing world. Further growth will be uneconomic because it will produce more social and environmental costs than it does benefits. Some argue (NEF, 2006; UNEP, 2011) that the only option is for 'green' growth that meets the dual objectives of economic growth and environmental protection with a focus on better outcomes not more outputs – a shift from quantity to quality. A transition towards a greener economy requires long-term sustainable growth and the efficient use of natural resources, reduction of carbon emissions, and eradication of poverty.

GDP has been used as a key indicator to measure the sum of all goods and services produced in a country over time. However, this national indicator of economic progress does not consider inequality, pollution or damage to people's health and the environment. Critics have called for GDP to be replaced with new indicators that better measure how our national policies can truly deliver a better quality of life for all within environmental limits (NEF, 2006). This will require the need to develop a new form of prosperity that is not dependent on continual growth (Jackson, 2009). Fundamental change to the structure of society and the market economy is needed if real environmental gains are to be achieved. Change on the scale achieved in the industrial revolution is required, which is driven by clean, efficient and sustainable renewable energy technologies (see Chapter Three).

All economic sectors will need to grow without undermining the capacity of the environment to support future quality of life. They will need to develop greater resilience to future environmental challenges such as climate change, material, energy and food insecurity and natural disasters. The 2011 UNEP published a report, *Towards a green economy*, which demonstrated that a transition to a green economy is possible by investing 2 per cent of global GDP per year (approximately

US$1.3 trillion) between now and 2050. This would involve a green transformation of key sectors, including agriculture, buildings, energy, fisheries, forests, manufacturing, tourism, transport, water and waste management. However, such investments must be spurred by national and international policy reforms (UNEP, 2011). It also argued that a green economy could be a catalyst for growth and poverty eradication in developing countries; where in some cases close to 90 per cent of the GDP of the poor is linked to nature or natural capital such as forests and freshwaters. To kickstart a transition towards a low carbon, resource efficient economy the report recommended prioritising government spending that stimulated green economic sectors and limiting spending on environmentally perverse subsidies that damage the environment.

The green economy in the context of sustainable development, poverty eradication and the institutional framework for sustainable development were the two main themes addressed by the United Nation Conference on Sustainable Development in Rio de Janeiro, Brazil in June 2012 (termed Rio+20). Rio+20 was criticised by many NGOs for failing to be forceful enough to meet the contemporary environment and development challenges. The global summit was seen as a missed opportunity to 're-energize the global conversation and importantly drive greater action around sustainability' (Monbiot, 2012). However, in the final document labelled *The future we want* the international community affirmed the need to achieve a green economy and advance sustainable development goals and support better governance of environmental issues (see Box 6.5). The green economy is acknowledged as an important factor in poverty eradication and assisting in sustainable management of natural resources with lower negative environmental impacts as well as increasing resource efficiency and reducing waste. The rhetoric contained in the final report of the conference will need to be matched by action with clear financial incentives to encourage greener investment and behaviour in government, businesses and consumers.

Box 6.5: The future we want

The outcome document of the 2012 Rio +20 Earth Summit called for a wide range of actions including:

- launching a process to establish sustainable development goals;
- detailing how the green economy can be used as a tool to achieve sustainable development;
- strengthening the UN Environment Programme and establishing a new forum for sustainable development;
- promoting corporate sustainability reporting measures;
- taking steps to go beyond GDP to assess the well-being of a country;
- developing a strategy for sustainable development financing;
- adopting a framework for tackling sustainable consumption and production;
- focusing on improving gender equality;
- stressing the need to engage civil society and incorporate science into policy; and
- recognising the importance of voluntary commitments on sustainable development.

Source: UNGA (2012)

Political will and public acceptance

As demonstrated in Chapter Five, a key challenge to addressing future environmental challenges will be political will. The vested interests of lobby groups and public acceptance of environmental policy measures influence the willingness of elected governments to adopt the radical measures necessary to make the transition to a sustainable low carbon society. Environmental scepticism generally, and climate scepticsm in particular, has been increasing. Environmental scepticism denies the seriousness of environmental problems, and 'sceptics' claim to be unbiased analysts combating 'junk science' (Jacques et al, 2008). The US conservative opposition to environmentalism has increased since the

1970s and has manifested itself in the form of conservative think tanks sponsored by corporate organisations and foundations. Conservative think tanks have coordinated an anti-environmental counter-movement that has successfully promoted environmental scepticism (Jacques et al, 2008). A prominent environmental sceptic is Bjorn Lomborg who challenges the priority given by public policy to environmental problems. He argues that environmental concerns are based on myths and warns: 'when we are told that something is a problem we need to ask how it is important in relation to other problems' (Lomborg, 2001, 9). While environmental scepticism is strongest in the USA, it is increasing in other parts of the world, especially with regard to climate change (Haq and Paul, 2012).

A Globescan poll showed that environmental concerns among citizens around the world have been falling since 2009 and reached a 20-year low in 2012. A total of nearly 23,000 citizens were interviewed across 22 countries. Fewer people consider air pollution, water pollution, species loss, motor vehicle emissions, fresh water shortages, and climate change as 'very serious' than at any time since polling began 20 years ago. Concern for climate change was, however, lower between 1998 to 2003. Concern about air and water pollution, as well as biodiversity, is significantly below where it was in the 1990s. Many of the sharpest falls took place in the period 2010–12 perhaps indicating the influence of the global economic crisis on public attitudes to the environment (Globescan, 2013).

The perceived seriousness of climate change has fallen particularly sharply since the 2009 UN Climate Summit in Copenhagen failed to agree legally binding greenhouse gas targets. Climate concern initially fell in industrialised countries, but 2012 figures show that concern fell in major developing economies such as Brazil and China. Despite the steep fall in environmental concern over the period 2009–12, majorities still consider most of these environmental problems to be 'very serious'. A total of 58 per cent of respondents considered water pollution as the most serious environmental problem while climate change was rated second least serious out of the six, with one in two (49 per cent) viewing it as 'very serious'.

The scientific evidence on the human impact on the global environment is increasing. However, the global economic crisis has resulted in an increased public fear of unemployment and a reduction in social services which are perceived as an immediate threat to wellbeing (unlike many environmental issues). There will always be vested interest groups opposed to changing the status quo. However, mobilising public opinion is vital for the revolutionary change needed to make the transition to a sustainable society. This is required if elected governments are to implement the policy measures necessary to make such a transition.

SUMMARY

- Population, income, production and consumption of products and services are the key drivers that have resulted in a wide range of environmental problems.
- The increasing interconnection between food, water and energy in combination with climate change will have far-reaching effects on global development.
- Meeting future environmental challenges will require more flexible and adaptive global and national governance frameworks and a redefinition of wealth and prosperity.
- A key challenge to addressing future environmental challenges will be political will and public acceptance.
- Mobilising public opinion is vital for the revolutionary change needed to make the transition to a sustainable society

READING GUIDE

Chatham House, 2012, Resource Futures, London: Chatham House, www.chathamhouse.org/sites/default/files/public/Research/Energy, per cent20Environment per cent20and per cent20Development/1212r_ resourcesfutures.pdf

Lynas, M, 2011, The God species: How the planet can survive the age of humans, London: Fourth Estate

NEF (New Economics Foundation), 2006, *Growth isn't working*, London: New Economics Foundation, http://www.neweconomics.org/ publications/entry/growth-isnt-possible

Rockström, J, Steffen, W, Noone, K et al, 2011, A safe operating space for humanity, Nature 461, 472–5

UNEP (United Nations Environment Programme), 2012, *Global Environment Outlook 5*, Nairobi: United Nations Environment Programme, www.unep.org/geo/geo5.asp

UNGA (United Nations General Assembly), 2012, The future we want, www.un.org/ga/search/view_doc.asp?symbol=A/RES/66/288&Lang=E

Zalasiewicz, J, Williams, M, Haywood, A, Ellis, M, 2011, The athropocene: A new epoch of geological time?, *Philosophical Transactions of the Royal Society A*, 369, 835–41

7

Conclusions

Introduction

This short guide has provided a brief introduction to environmental policy and how contemporary environmental issues have an impact on human health and wellbeing. It has examined the various socio-economic perspectives that exist with regard to our understanding of environmental issues and how they relate to the formulation and implementation of environmental policies. It has also discussed the different approaches to tackling specific environmental issues at the international, national and local level. The last two chapters have highlighted some of the challenges to environmental management and issues that are likely to shape future environmental policy. This guide has shown the complex nature of environmental policy development and implementation, especially in the context of scientific uncertainty, growing public scepticism, and the tensions between long-term environmental effects and the short-term nature of decision-making. This final chapter summarises some of the main themes discussed, reiterating key environmental problems, policy responses and challenges.

Key problems

In developed countries industrialisation is widely regarded as having contributed to the acceleration of environmental change. Our awareness and understanding of humanity's impact on the environment have increased in the post-war period. New social movements, political parties, greater media coverage of environmental disasters, and a growing body of scientific evidence on the effects of environmental pollution have all led to an increased imperative to take action. This increased environmental awareness and concern is reflected in the number of international conferences and conventions that took place from the 1970s onwards. Some of the most influential publications were written during this period, especially the 1987 Brundtland report which attempted to define sustainable development, a concept (and definition) that has never been replaced as the dominant paradigm despite its usefulness to policy making being criticised.

However, the environmental impact of developed countries is only half of the policy problem. Countries such as China and India are now undergoing rapid development, industrialisation and motorisation and are subsequently witnessing profound environmental changes. These changes have a negative social impact on local populations and contribute to global environmental problems such as climate change. A major policy challenge is how to address these issues. While countries such as the USA have argued within climate change negotiations that rapidly developing/industrialised economies should be required to commit to limiting their carbon emissions, countries such as India and China have responded that it is unfair that development should be limited. Climate change is one of the largest areas of environmental policy at present, although similar arguments are used when debating biodiversity conservation and protecting natural resources in developing countries.

The human cost of environmental change must not be underestimated. Chapter Two highlighted the health effects of air pollution and the negative effects of land degradation in terms of reduced crop productivity and food security. The consequences of many social changes, for example, population growth and an increased trend towards urbanisation have all had social and environmental consequences. The loss of arable land has increased concerns about food security, and has contributed to higher levels of environmental pollution. Poor sanitation in developing countries, especially in slum areas on the peripheries of cities is clearly associated with an increase in preventable, yet fatal diseases such as cholera. Additionally, conflicts and social unrest associated with dwindling resources are evident, and are likely to increase if current trends continue.

The impact of climate change is potentially so profound that it deserves separate attention here. Possible population displacement, widespread threats to those living in low lying areas, risks to food security, increased diseases are all predicted impacts of climate change. While the immediate burden of these effects are more likely to fall on developing countries (both as a result of geographic factors *and* resilience to them), there are major implications also for developed nations.

Key responses

In order to effectively address environmental problems through policy, a number of issues needed to be considered:

- balancing social, economic and environmental objectives
- addressing uncertainty, risk and the negative impacts of policies
- the scale of the problem and the solution.

Traditionally, environmental policy has had to compete with social and economic objectives. While sustainable development has provided the paradigm to demonstrate that all three are equally important, this has has not always been translated into practice. Attempts have been made, however, to include the environmental costs of human activity into policy evaluation tools by giving a monetary value to the costs and benefits of environmental regulation.

At the international level, policy debates have attempted to balance economic and development concerns. One of the strategies of international climate policy is the investment in projects that will encourage greener development trajectories in developing countries. Although, this has also been criticised by some as developed countries 'paying to pollute', and that by investing in low carbon development elsewhere domestic norms and behaviours are not substantially addressed.

Responding to inequalities resulting from environmental problems (both human driven and natural) has also been an important theme. At the international level, it is clear that questions of fairness pervade climate negotiations and in many respects have prevented further action. Equally, when considering the suitability of policy instruments at the national and local policy levels concerns are often raised about the impact of certain measures on the poorest sections of society who may be disproportionately affected.

Dealing with uncertainty, risk and the negative impacts of policies

The balance between uncertainty and risk is another key factor that influences the formulation of environmental policy. Sociologists have attempted to understand the nature of the environment, the construction of risk and scientific evidence. Indeed, it is clear from the debates considered in this guide that policy is not a linear process where an environmental problem and its causes are discovered by scientists, and solutions put in place by policy makers. In some instances, public and media concerns about risks have shaped policy more than scientific evidence, in others, scientific uncertainty has been used by political elites as a reason to delay action that might be politically unpopular and economically costly, regardless of the precautionary principle.

The scale of the problem and the solution

Environmental problems occur at a range of levels, and are likely to have diverse effects on different people, communities, regions and countries. The increasing interconnection between food, water and energy in combination with climate change will have far-reaching effects on global development. This requires policy responses at all levels. Each policy level has different challenges. International policy making is fraught with difficulty when seeking consensus between diverse and often competing political agendas. Equally, national level policy making is influenced partly by external drivers such as international policy, but also issues such as the national political system, national elites, existing policy frameworks or legacies, and any national level environmental concerns. Local level policy is affected by many similar issues, but is often subject to local circumstances such as specific environmental problems or controversies.

Future challenges

Meeting future environmental challenges will require more flexible and adaptive global and national governance frameworks. Doing so will also potentially require a redefinition of wealth and prosperity, taking into account the impact of consuming limited and non-renewable resources. Potential barriers to meeting these challenges may include a lack of political will to make difficult changes with short-term costs, and a lack of public acceptance that such changes are necessary. In developed countries, popular aspirations, habits and lifestyles which rely on high levels of consumption may not be amenable to the action that is needed to address environmental challenges, suggesting the requirement for change in some aspects of society and social norms. A further challenge is the requirement to consider the economic development needs of the world's poorest countries alongside the need for environmental protection.

Final thoughts

Humanity is facing increased natural resource scarcity, rising global temperatures, biodiversity loss, environmental pollution and food and energy insecurity. Appropriate and effective environmental policy is necessary if we are to remain within planetary boundaries and ensure the future survival of humankind.

References

Abels, G, 2005, The long and winding road from Asilomar to Brussels: Science, politics and the public in biotechnology regulation, *Science as Culture* 14, 4, 339–53

Ackerman, F, 2009, Can we afford the future? The economics of a warming world, London: Zed Books, p 12

Agyeman, J (2002) Constructing environmental (in)justice: transatlantic tales, *Environmental Politics,* 11, 3: 1-53.

Ahmed, SA, Diffenbaugh, NS, Whertel, T, 2009, Climate volatility deepens poverty vulnerability in developing countries, *Environmental Research Letters* 4, 3

Alberini, A, Segerson, K, 2002, Assessing voluntary programs to improve environmental quality, Environmental and Resource Economics 22, 157–84

Australian Greenhouse Office, 2006, *Evaluation of Australian TravelSmart projects in the ACT, South Australia, Queensland, Victoria and Western Australia 2001–2005*, Canberra: Department of Environment and Heritage, www.travelsmart.gov.au/publications/pubs/evaluation-2005.pdf

Backhaus, JG, 2004, Increasing the role of environmental taxes and charges as a policy instrument in developing countries, *American Journal of Economics and Sociology* 63, 5, 1097–130

Baker, S, 2006, *Sustainable development*, London: Routledge

Bang, G, Hovi, J, Sprinz, DF, 2012, US presidents and the failure to ratify multilateral environmental agreements, *Climate Policy* 12, 6, 755–63

Barr, S, Gilg, AW, Shaw, G, 2011, 'Helping people make better choices': Exploring the behaviour change agenda for environmental sustainability, *Applied Geography* 31, 712–20

Barrett, S, 1998, On the theory and diplomacy of environmental treaty-making, *Environmental and Resource Economics* 11, 3–4, 317–33

Baumgartner, FR and Jones, BD, 1993, *Agendas and instability in American politics*, Chicago: University of Chicago Press

BBC, 2011, Reaction to UN climate deal, www.bbc.co.uk/news/science-environment-16129762

BBC, 2013, Fracking protests: Green MP Caroline Lucas arrested near Balcombe, West Sussex, 19 August, www.bbc.co.uk/news/uk-england-23759827

Bedford, T, Jones, P, Walker, H, 2004, *'Every little bit helps': Overcoming the challenges to researching and promoting and implementing sustainable lifestyles*, London: Centre of Sustainable Development, University of Westminster

Bell, D, Gray, T, Haggett, C, 2005, The 'social gap' in wind farm siting decisions: Explanations and policy responses, *Environmental Politics* 14, 4, 460–77

Bennulf, M, 1995, The rise and fall of Miljopartiet de Grona, in D Richardson and C Rootes (eds) *The Green challenge: The development of Green parties in Europe*, London: Routledge, pp 128–46

Benton, T, 1994, Biology and social theory in the environmental debate, in M Redclift, T Benton (eds) *Social theory and the global environment*, London: Routledge

Benton, T, Redclift, M, 1994, Introduction, in M Redclift, T Benton (eds) *Social theory and the global environment*, London: Routledge

Bingham, N, Blackmore, R, 2003, What to do? How risk and uncertainty affect environmental responses, in S Hinchliffe, A Blowers, J Freeland (eds) *Understanding environmental issues*, Milton Keynes: Open University, pp 127–64

BMA (British Medical Association), 2012, *Healthy transport = healthy lives*, http://bma.org.uk/transport

Bodansky, DM, 1999, The legitimacy of international governance: A coming challenge for international environmental law?, *Scholarly Works*, Paper 443, http://digitalcommons.law.uga.edu/fac_artchop/443

Bodansky, DM, 2011, W(h)ither the Kyoto Protocol? Durban and beyond, Harvard project on climate agreements, http://papers.ssrn.com/sol3/papers.cfm?abstract_id=1917603

Borkey, P, Leveque, F, 2000, Voluntary approaches for environmental protection in the European Union – a survey, *European Environment* 10, 1, 35–54

Boulding, KE, The economics of the coming spaceship Earth, in H Jarrett (ed.), *Environmental quality in a growing economy*, Baltimore: Johns Hopkins University Press, 1966: 3-14.

Bourdieu, P, 1984, *Distinction: A social critique of the Judgement of Taste*, London: Routledge

BP (British Petroleum), 2013, *Energy outlook 2012*, London: BP

Brand, S, 2009, *Whole earth discipline: An ecopragmatist manifesto*, London: Viking

Bróg, W, Erl, E, Mense, N, 2002, Individualised marketing: Changing travel behavior for a better environment, Paper presented at the OECD Workshop: Environmentally sustainable transport, 5–6 December 2002, Socialdata, www.socialdata.de/info/IndiMark.pdf

Brohe, A, Eyre, N, Howarth, N, 2009, *Carbon markets: An international business guide*, London: Earthscan

Brouhle, K, Griffiths, C, Wolverton, A, 2009, Evaluating the role of EPA policy levers: An examination of a voluntary program and regulatory threat in the metal-finishing industry, *Journal of Environmental Economics and Management* 57, 2, 166–81

Bullard, R, 1999, Dismantling environmental racism in the USA, *Local Environment: The International Journal of Justice and Sustainability* 4, 1, 5–19

Bullock, S, Cottray, O, McLaren, D, Pipes, S, Taylor, M, 2000, *Quality of life counts: Where next?*, London: Friends of the Earth, www.foe.co.uk/campaigns/sustainabledevelopment/publications/qolc_0200.html

Burningham, K, 2000, Using the Language of NIMBY: A topic for research, not an activity for researchers, *Local Environment: The International Journal of Justice and Sustainability* 5, 1, 55–67

Busch, P-O, Jörgens, H, 2005, The international sources of policy convergence: Explaining the spread of environmental policy innovations, *Journal of European Public Policy* 12, 860–84

Cahill, M, 2002, The environment and social policy, London: Routledge

Campbell, C, 1998, Consuming goods and the good of consuming, in DA Crocker, T Linden (eds) *Ethics of consumption: The good life, justice, and global stewardship*, Lanham, MD: Rowman & Littlefield

Canadell JG, Le Quéré C, Raupach MR, Field CB, Buitenhuis ET, Ciais P, Conway TJ, Gillett NP, Houghton RA, Marland G, 2007, Contributions to accelerating atmospheric CO2 growth from economic activity, carbon intensity, and efficiency of natural sinks, *Proceedings of the National Academy of Sciences,* 104: 18866–70, doi 10.1073_pnas.0702737104

Carson, R, 1962 *Silent spring,* New York: Houghton Mifflin Company

Carter, N, 2007, *The politics of the environment,* 2nd edn, Cambridge: Cambridge University Press

Carter, N, Ockwell, D, 2007, *New labour, new environment? An analysis of the Labour government's policy on climate change and biodiversity loss,* Report prepared for Friends of the Earth, London, http://celp.org.uk/webpages/projects/foe/fullreportfinal.pdf http://celp.org.uk/webpages/projects/foe/fullreportfinal.pdf

Castells, N, Ravetz, J, 2001, Science and policy in international environmental agreements, *International environmental agreements: Politics, law and economics* 1, 405–25

CBS News, 2011, Canada pulls out of, denounces Kyoto Protocol, www.cbsnews.com/8301-202_162-57341907/canada-pulls-out-of-denounces-kyoto-protocol/

CFS (Committee on Food Security), 2012, *Executive summary of the high-level panel of experts report on social protection and food security,* Committee on World Security, Rome: Committee on Food Security

Chan, CK, Yao, X, 2008, Air pollution in mega cities in China, *Atmospheric Environment* 42, 1–42

Chaney, D, 1996, *Lifestyles,* London: Routledge

Charles, G, 2010, Act on CO$_2$ voted best green online campaign, *Marketing Magazine,* www.marketingmagazine.co.uk/news/983666/

Chasek, P, Downie, D, Brown, J, 2006, *Global environmental politics,* 4th edn, Boulder, CO: Westview Press

Chatham House, 2012, Resource futures, London: Chatham House, www.chathamhouse.org/sites/default/files/public/Research/Energy,%20Environment%20and%20Development/1212r_resourcesfutures.pdf

Chatterton, P, Style, S, 2001, Putting sustainable development into practice? The role of local policy partnership networks, *Local Environment* 6, 4, 439–52

Connelly, J, Smith, G, 1999, *Politics and the environment,* London: Routledge

Corner, A, Randall, A, 2011, Selling climate change? The limitations of social marketing as a strategy for climate change public engagement, *Global Environmental Change* 21, 1005–14

Costanza, R, d'Arge, R, de Groot, R et al, 1987, The value of the world's ecosystem services and natural capital, Nature 387, 253–60

Crompton, T, Thøgersen, J, 2009, *Simple and painless? The limitations of spillover in environmental campaigning*, Godalming: Worldwide Fund for Nature

Daily Mail, 2012, The great Easter get nowhere: RAC warns that petrol panic buying risks millions of drivers not being able to fill their tanks for holiday break, 29 March, www.dailymail.co.uk/news/article-2121984/Petrol-strike-Fuel-crisis-panic-buying-puts-Easter-holiday-drivers-greater-risk-shortages.html

Daly, HE, 2008, A steady-state economy, London: Sustainable Development Commission

Danaher, M, 2002, Why Japan will not give up whaling, Pacific Review: Peace, Security and Global Change 14, 2, 105–20

Darnall, N, Potoski, P, Prakash, A, 2010, Sponsorship matters: Assessing business participation in government- and industry-sponsored voluntary environmental programs, Journal of Public Administration Research and Theory 20, 2, 283–307

Dean, J, Lovely, M, Wang, H, 2009, Are foreign investors attracted to weak environmental regulations? Evaluating the evidence from China, *Journal of Development Economics* 90, 1, 1–13

Deese, RS, 2009, The artefact of nature: 'Spaceship Earth' and the dawn of global environmentalism', *Endeavour* 33, 2, 70–5

Defra (Department for Environment, Food and Rural Affairs), 2011, *Biodiversity strategy 2020*, www.defra.gov.uk/publications/files/pb13583-biodiversity-strategy-2020-111111.pdf

Defra (Department for Environment, Food and Rural Affairs), 2013, *Sustainable government regional summaries*, http://archive.defra.gov.uk/sustainable/government/progress/regional/summaries/images/60NE_001.gif

DfT (Department for Transport), 2012, *Road accidents and safety quarterly estimates*, www.gov.uk/government/uploads/system/uploads/attachment_data/file/9286/road-accidents-and-safety-quarterly-estimates-q2-2012.pdf

Dietz, TE, Ostrom, E, Stern, PC, 2003, The struggle to govern the commons, *Science* 302, 1907–12

Docherty, I, Shaw, J, 2008, *Traffic jam: Ten years of 'sustainable' transport in the UK*, Bristol: Policy Press

Downie, D, 2011, Global environmental policy: Governance through regimes, in RS Axelrod, SD VanDeveer, DL Downie (eds) *The global environment: Institutions, law and policy*, Washington, DC: CQ Press

Downs, A, 1972, Up and down with ecology: The issue–attention cycle, Public Interest 28, Summer, 38–50

DTI (Department of Trade and Industry), 2001, *UK fuel poverty strategy*, London: HMSO, www.decc.gov.uk/en/content/cms/funding/fuel_poverty/strategy/strategy.aspx

Dunlap, RE, 2010, The maturation and diversification of environmental sociology: From constructivism and realism to agnosticism and pragmatism, in M Redclift, G Woodgate (eds) *The international handbook of environmental sociology*, 2nd edn, Cheltenham: Edward Elgar

Dyson, T, 1996, *Population and food: Global trends and future prospects*, London: Routledge

The Ecologist (1972) *A blue print for survival*, Penguin

EIA (Energy Information Administration), 2012, International energy statistics, www.eia.gov/cfapps/ipdbproject/IEDIndex3.cfm

Ehrlich, PR, Ehrlich, AH, 2009, The population bomb revisited, *The Electronic Journal of Sustainable Development* 1, 3, 63–71

European Environment Agency, 2013, *Celebrating Europe and its environment*, www.eea.europa.eu/environmental-time-line/

Evans, A, 2010, *Globalization and scarcity: Multilaterism for a word with limits*, New York: Center on International Cooperation, New York University

FAO (Food and Agriculture Organization of the United Nations), 2006, *Livestock a major threat to the environment*, www.fao.org/newsroom/en/news/2006/1000448/index.html

FAO (Food and Agriculture Organization of the United Nations), 2009, Farming must change to feed the world, Press Release, 4 February, www.fao.org/news/story/jp/item/9962/icode/

FAO (Food and Agriculture Organization of the United Nations), 2012a, *Food security and climate change*, Rome: FAO, www.fao.org/fileadmin/user_upload/hlpe/hlpe_documents/HLPE_Reports/HLPE-Report-3-Food_security_and_climate_change-June_2012.pdf

FAO (Food and Agriculture Organization of the United Nations), 2012b, *Towards the future we want: End hunger and make the transition to sustainable agricultural and food systems*, Rome: FAO

FAO (Food and Agriculture Organization of the United Nations), 2013, *Farming must change to feed the world*, www.fao.org/news/story/en/item/9962/icode/

Fell, D, Austin, A, Kivinen, E, Wilkins, C, 2009, *The diffusion of environmental behaviours: The role of influential Individuals in social networks*, London: Brook Lyndhurst, Defra

Fitzpatrick, T (ed), 2011, *Understanding the environment and social policy*, Bristol: Policy Press

Fitzpatrick, T, Cahill, M (eds), 2002, *Environment and welfare*, Basingstoke: Palgrave Macmillan

FoE (Friends of the Earth), 1999, *The geographic relation between household income and polluting factories*, London: FoE, www.foe.co.uk/resource/reports/income_pollution.html

FoE (Friends of the Earth), 2007, Brief history of The Big Ask: Friends of the Earth's climate campaign, July, London: FoE, www.foe.co.uk/resource/media_briefing/brief_history_the_big_ask.pdf

Folke, C, Hahn, T, Olsson, P, Norberg, J, 2005, Adaptive governance of social-ecological systems, *Annual Review of Environment and Resources* 30, 441–73

Ford-Thompson, AES, Snell, CJ, Saunders, G, White, PCL, 2012, Stakeholder participation in management of invasive vertebrates, *Conservation Biology* 26, 2, 345–56

Forestry Commission, 2013, *Carbon sequestration*, www.forestry.gov.uk/forestry/infd-7m8fge

Galbraith, JK, 1999, The affluent society, London: Penguin Books, pp 101

Gelderblom, D, Kok, P, 1994, *Urbanisation: South Africa's challenge. Vol 1: Dynamics*, Pretoria: HSRC Press

Geller, ES, 1989, Applied behavior analysis and social marketing: An integration for environmental preservation, *Journal of Social Issues* 45, 1, 17–36

Georgescu-Roegen, N, 1976, Energy and economic myths, New York: Pergamon Press, pp xix

Georgescu-Roegen, N, 1971, *The entropy law and the economic process*, Cambridge, MA: Harvard University Press

Global Humanitarian Assistance, 2012, *Bangladesh country briefing*, www.globalhumanitarianassistance.org/wp-content/uploads/2012/01/Bangladesh-country-briefing.pdf

Globescan, 2013, *Environmental concerns at record lows: Global-poll*, www.globescan.com/commentary-and-analysis/press-releases/press-releases-2013/261-environmental-concerns-at-record-lows-global-poll.html

Godfray, HCJ, Crute, IR, Haddad, L et al, 2010, The future of the global food system, *Philosophical Transactions of the Royal Society B*, 365, 2769–77

Gough, I, 2011, Climate change and public policy futures: A report prepared for the British Academy, London: British Academy Policy Centre

Gough, I, 2012, *New policies are needed to reconcile climate mitigation and social equity in the UK*, http://blogs.lse.ac.uk/politicsandpolicy/2012/03/29/climate-mitigation-social-equity-gough/

Gough, I, Marden, S, 2011, Fiscal costs of climate mitigation programmes in the UK: A challenge for social policy, *Centre for Analysis of Social Exclusion*, Working Paper 145, London: CASE

Gough, I, Meadowcroft, J, 2011, Decarbonising the welfare state, in JS Dryzek, RB Norgaard, D Schlosberg (eds) *Oxford handbook of climate change and society*, Oxford: Oxford University Press

Gough, I, Meadowcroft, J, Dryzek, J et al, 2008, JESP symposium: Climate change and social policy, *Journal of European Social Policy* 18, 4, 325–44

Gowdy, J, Mesner, S, 1998, The evolution of Georgescu-Roegen's bioeconomics, *Review of Social Economy* 56, 2, 136–56

Greener, I, 2005, State of the art: The potential of path dependence in political studies, *Politics* 25, 1, 62–72

Gronco, J, Warde, A, 2001 *Ordinary consumption*, London: Routledge

Guardian, 2000, Toxic shock, Friday 11 February, www.guardian.co.uk/theguardian/2000/feb/11/features11.g2

Guardian, 2010, Climate change adverts help take debate among public back several years, www.guardian.co.uk/environment/blog/2010/mar/17/climate-change-advertising-standards-authority

Gulbrandsen, LH, 2010, *Transnational environmental governance: The emergence and effects of the certification of forests and fisheries*, Gloucester: Edward Elgar

Hall, PA, 1993, Policy paradigms, social learning, and the state: The case of economic policy-making in Britain, *Comparative Politics* 25, 3, 275–96

Hanley, N, Barbier, EB, 2009, Pricing nature: Cost–benefit analysis and environmental policy, Cheltenham: Edward Elgar

Hannigan, J, 2006, *Environmental sociology: A social constructionist perspective*, 2nd edn, London: Routledge

Haq, G, Paul, A, 2012, *Environmentalism since 1945*, London: Routledge

Haq, G, Whitelegg, J, Cinderby, S, Owen, A, 2008, The use of personalised social marketing to foster voluntary behavioural change for sustainable travel and lifestysles, *Local Environment* 13, 7, 549–69

Haq, G, Snell, C, Gutman, G, Brown, D, 2013, *Global ageing and environmental change: Attitudes, risks and opportunities*, York: Stockholm Environment Institute

Hardin, G, 1968, The tragedy of the commons, *Science* 162, 3859, 1243–8

Hards, S, 2011, Social practice and the evolution of personal environmental values, *Environmental Values* 20, 1, 23–42

Hards, S, 2012, Tales of transformation: The potential of a narrative approach to pro-environmental practices, *Geoforum* 43, 4, 760–71

Harvey, D, 2006, The limits to capital, Verso, London, pp 334–35

Haythornthwaite, C, 1996, Social network analysis: An approach and technique for the study of information exchange, *Library and Information Science Research* 18, 323–42

HCTC (House of Commons Treasury Committee), 2008, *Climate change and the Stern review: The implications for Treasury policy*, Fourth Report of Session 2007–08, London: House of Commons Treasury Committee, TSO

Heiskanen, E, Johnson, M, Robinson, S, Vadovics, E, Saastamoinen, M, 2010, Low-carbon communities as a context for individual behaviour change, *Energy Policy* 38, 7586–95

Hermann, IT, Hauschild, MZ, 2009, Effects of globalisation on carbon footprints of products, *CIRP Annals: Manufacturing Technology* 58, 1, 13–16

Hey, C, 2005, EU environmental policies: a short history of the policy strategies, www.eeb.org/publication/chapter-3.pdf

Higgins, P, Chan, K, Porder, S, 2006, Bridge over a philosophical divide, *Evidence and Policy: A Journal of Research, Debate and Practice* 2, 2, 249–55

Hill, M, 2009, The Policy Process, 5th edn, Harlow: Pearson

Hinchliffe, S, 1996, Helping the earth begins at home: The social construction of socio-environmental responsibilities, *Global Environmental Change* 6, 1, 53–62

Hobson, K, 2003, Thinking habits into action: The role of knowledge and process in questioning household consumption practices, *Local Environment* 8, 1, 95–112

Holdsworth, M, Steedman, P, 2005, *16 pain-free ways to save the planet*, London: National Consumer Council, www.ncc.org.uk/responsibleconsumption/16ways.pdf

Home, R, (2007) A short guide to European law papers in land management, no. 4, Anglia Ruskin University

House of Commons Library, 2012, *Shale gas and fracking*, Standard Note SN/SC/6073, London: House of Commons Library

Hovi, J, Spingz, DF, Underdal, A, 2009, Implementing long-term climate policy: Time inconsistency, domestic politics, international anarchy, *Global Environmental Politics* 9, 3, 20–39

Hubacek, K, Guan, D, Barrett, J, Wiedmann, T, 2009, Environmental implications of urbanization and lifestyle change in China: Ecological and water footprints, *Journal of Cleaner Production* 17, 1241–8

Huby, M, 1998, *Social policy and the environment*, Oxford: Oxford University Press

Hudson, J, Lowe, S, 2009, *Understanding the policy process: Analysing welfare policy and practice*, 2nd edn, Bristol: Policy Press

Hudson, J, Lowe, S, Kuhner, S, 2008, *The short guide to social policy*, Bristol: Policy Press

Hulme, M, 2010, *Why we disagree about climate change*, Cambridge: Cambridge University Press

Hyde, FE, 1971, *Liverpool and the Mersey: An economic history of a port, 1700–1970*, Newton Abbot: David and Charles

IEA (International Energy Agency), 2012a, *World Energy Outlook 2012*, Vienna: IEA

IEA (International Energy Agency), 2012b, *Global carbon-dioxide emissions increase by 1.0 Gt in 2011 to record high*, www.iea.org/newsroomandevents/news/2012/may/name,27216,en.html

IISD (International Institute for Sustainable Development), 2012, *Sustainable development timeline*, www.iisd.org/pdf/2012/sd_timeline_2012.pdf

The Independent Commission on International Development Issues (1980) *North-South: A programme for survival*, Pan Books, London

Involve/DEA, 2010, *Nudge, think, or shove? Shifting values and attitudes towards sustainability: A briefing for sustainability practitioners*, www.involve. org.uk/wp-content/uploads/2011/03/Nudge-think-or-shove.pdf

IPCC (Intergovernmental Panel on Climate Change), 1990, *Climate change: The IPCC scientific assessment (1990)*, www.ipcc.ch/publications_ and_data/publications_ipcc_first_assessment_1990_wg1.shtml#. Uo9KZCcva8B

IPCC (Intergovernmental Panel on Climate Change), 1995, *The science of climate change: Contribution of Working Group I to the Second Assessment Report of the Intergovernmental Panel on Climate Change*, Cambridge: Cambridge University Press

IPCC (Intergovernmental Panel on Climate Change), 2001, *Climate Change 2001: Synthesis report*, www.ipcc.ch/ipccreports/tar/vol4/english/

IPCC (Intergovernmental Panel on Climate Change), 2007a, *Climate change 2007. Working Group II: Impacts, Adaptation and Vulnerability*, www. ipcc.ch/publications_and_data/ar4/wg2/en/ch5s5-4-2.html

IPCC (Intergovernmental Panel on Climate Change), 2007b, *The physical science basis, Contribution of Working Group I to the Fourth Assessment Report of the Intergovernmental Panel on Climate Change*, Cambridge: Cambridge University Press

IPCC (International Panel for Climate Change), 2012a, *Organization*, www. ipcc.ch/organization/organization.shtml#.UCej_aCoqSo

IPCC (Intergovernmental Panel on Climate Change), 2012b, *Special Report on Managing the Risks of Extreme Events and Disasters to Advance Climate Change Adaptation, Intergovernmental Panel on Climate Change*, Cambridge: Cambridge University Press

IPCC (International Panel for Climate Change) 2013, Climate change 2013: the physical science basis, www.climatechange2013.org/

Irwin, A, 2001, *Sociology and the environment: A critical introduction to society, nature and knowledge*, Oxford: Polity

IUCN (International Union for Conservation of Nature), 2012, *More highlights from the latest IUCN update*, www.iucnredlist.org/news/more-highlights-from-the-latest-iucn-rl-update

Jackson, T, 2005, *Motivating sustainable consumption: A review of evidence on consumer behaviour and behavioural change*, London: Sustainable Development Research Network, www.sd-research. org.uk/sites/default/files/publications/Motivating%20Sustainable%20 Consumption1_0.pdf

Jackson, T, 2009, Prosperity without growth: Economics for a finite planet, London: Earthscan

Jacques, P, Dunlap, R, and Freeman, M. 2008, The organisation of denial: Conservative think tanks and environmental scepticism, *Environmental Politics*, 17, 3, 349–85

Japan Daily Press, 2012, Three thousand still missing in Japan after tsunami, http://japandailypress.com/three-thousand-still-missing-in-japan-after-tsunami-1111799

Jephcote, C, Chen, H, 2011, Environmental injustices of children's exposure to air pollution from road-transport within the model British multicultural city of Leicester: 2000–09, *Science of the Total Environment* 1, 141, 140–51

Jordan, A, Lorenzoni, I, 2007, Is there now a political climate for policy change? Policy and politics after the Stern review, *The Political Quarterly* 78, 2, 310–19

Jordan, A, Wurzel, RKW, Zito, AR, 2003a, 'New' instruments of environmental governance: Patterns and pathways of change, *Environmental Politics* 12, 1, 3–24

Jordan, A, Wurzel, RKW, Zito, AR, 2003b, 'New' environmental policy instruments: An evolution or a revolution in environmental policy?, *Environmental Politics* 12, 1, 201–24

Jordan, A, Wurzev, RKW, Zito, AR, Brukner, L, 2003c, Policy innovation or muddling through? New environmental policy instruments in the UK, *Environmental Politics*, 12, 1, 179–200

Juniper, T, 2013, Counting the consequences, Ecologist, www.theecologist. org/magazine/features/1766176/counting_the_consequences.html

Kasser, T, Cohn, S, Kanner, AD, Ryan, RM, 2007, Some of the costs of American corporate capitalism: A psychological exploration of value and goals conflicts, *Psychological Inquiry* 18, 1–22

Kassirer, J, McKenzie-Mohr, D, 1998, *Tools change: Proven methods for promoting environmental citizenship*, Ottawa: National Round Table on Environment and Economy

Kathuria,V, 2006, Controlling water pollution in developing and transition countries: Lessons from three successful cases, *Journal of Environmental Management* 78, 4, 405-26

Kelemen, RD, Vogel, D, 2010, Trading places: The role of the United States and the European Union in international environmental politics, *Comparative Political Studies* 43, 427

Keys, T, and Malnight, T, 2012, The global trends report 2012, www.globaltrends.com/reports/gt-2012

Kharas, H, 2010, The emerging middle class in developing countries, *Working Paper* 285, Paris: OECD Development Centre

Knill, C, Debus, M, Heichel, S, 2010, Do parties matter in internationalised policy areas? The impact of political parties on environmental policy outputs in 18 OECD countries, 1970–2000, *The European Journal of Political Research* 49, 3, 301–36

Konig, T, Luetgert, B, 2008, Troubles with transposition? Explaining trends in member-state notification and the delayed transposition of EU directives, *British Journal of Political Studies* 39, 163–94

Kotler, P, Roberto, EL, 1989, Social marketing: Strategies for changing public behavior, New York: Free Press and Macmillan

Kraft, ME, Clary, BB, 1990, Citizen participation and the Nimby syndrome: Public response to radioactive waste disposal, *Western Political Quarterly* 44, 2, 299–328

Langhelle, O, 2000, Why ecological modernization and sustainable development should not be conflated, *Journal of Environmental Policy and Planning* 2, 303–22

Langton, J, 1983, Liverpool and its hinterland in the late eighteenth century, in BL Anderson and PMS Stoney (eds) *Commerce, industry and transport: Studies in economic change on Merseyside*, Liverpool: Liverpool University Press

Leitman, J, 2001, Integrating the environment in urban development: Singapore as a model of good practice, *Urban Waste Management Working Paper* Series 7, Washington DC: Urban Development Division, World Bank

Lele, S, 1991, Sustainable development: A critical review, *World Development* 19, 6, 607–21

Levy, MA, Young, OR, Ziirn, M, 1994, The study of international regimes 1994, *Working Paper*, www.iiasa.ac.at/Publications/Documents/WP-94-113.pdf

Liddick, DR, 2006, *Eco-terrorism, radical environmental and animal liberation movements*, Westport, CT: Praeger

Lidskog, R, Sundquvist, G, 2002, The role of science in environmental regimes: The Case of LRTAP, *European Journal of International Relations* 8, 1, 77–101

Lomborg, B, 2001, *The skeptical environmentalist*, Cambridge: Cambridge University Press

Lorek, S, Spangenberg, JH, 2001, Indicators for environmental sustainable household consumption, *International Journal of Sustainable Development* 4, 1, 101–19

Lowe, P, Ward, S (eds), 1998, *British environmental policy and Europe: Politics and policy in transition*, London: Routledge

Luke, WT, 2005, Neither sustainable nor development: Reconsidering sustainability in development, *Sustainable Development* 13, 228–38

Lynas, M, 2011, The God species: How the planet can survive the age of humans, London: Fourth Estate

McClaren, N, 1998, Citizens' initiatives on sustainable consumption, Workshop on encouraging local initiatives towards sustainable consumption patterns, 2–4 February 1998 Vienna, Austria, Geneva: United Nations Economic Commission for Europe, www.unece.org/env/europe/workshop/macllaren.e.pdf

McCormick, J, 1989, The global environmental movement, London: Belhaven Press.

McKenzie-Mohr, D, 2000, Fostering sustainable behavior through community-based social marketing, *American psychologist*, 55, 5, 531–37

McKenzie-Mohr, D, Smith, W, 1999, *Fostering sustainable behavior*, Gabriola Island, Canada: New Society

McLaughlin, P, Dietz, T, 2008, Structure, agency and environment: Toward an integrated perspective on vulnerability, *Global Environmental Change* 18, 99–111

Macnaghten, P, Urry, J, 1995, Towards a sociology of nature, *Sociology* 29, 2, 203–20

Makokha, AO, Mghweno, LR, Magoha, HS, Nakajugo, A, Wekesa, JM, 2008, Environmental lead pollution and contamination in food around Lake Victoria, Kisumu, Kenya, *African Journal of Environmental Science and Technology* 2 , 10, 349–53

Manney, G. L., M. L. Santee, M. Rex., N. J. Livesey, M. C. Pitts, P. Veefkind, E. R. Nash, I. Wohltmann, R. Lehmann, L. Froidevaux, L. R. Poole, M. R. Schoeberl, D. P. Haffner, J. Davies, V. Dorokhov, H. Gernandt, B. Johnson, R. Kivi, E. Kyrö, N. Larsen, P. F. Levelt, A. Makshtas, C. T. McElroy, H. Nakajima, M. C. Parrondo, D. W. Tarasick, P. von der Gathen, K. A. Walker and N. S. Zinoviev, 2011, Unprecedented Arctic ozone loss in 2011 echoed the Antarctic ozone hole. *Nature*, 478, 469-475

Marinelli, PA, Roth, MT, 2002, Travesmart suburbs Brisbane: A cast study of individualized marketing, *Papers of the Australasian Transport Research Forum*, 23, 2, 703–19

Marmot Review Team, 2010, *'Fair society healthy lives': Strategic review of health inequalities in England post 2010*, (The Marmot Review) www.instituteofhealthequity.org/projects/fair-society-healthy-lives-the-marmot-review

MEA (Millennium Ecosystem Assessment), 2005, Ecosystems and human wellbeing: Synthesis, Washington, DC: Island Press

Meadowcroft, J, 2000, Sustainable development: a new(ish) idea for a new century?, *Political Studies*, 48, 2, pages 370–87

Meadows, DH, Meadows, DL, Randers, J, Behrens III, WW, 1972, *The limits to growth*, New York: Universe Books.

Mill, JS, 1970, Principles of political economy, London: Penguin, p 111

MIT (Massachusetts Institute of Technology), 1970, Man's impact on the global environment: Assessment and recommendations for action, Cambridge, MA: MIT

Monbiot, G, 2012, Rio+20 draft text is 283 paragraphs of fluff, www.guardian.co.uk/environment/georgemonbiot/2012/jun/22/rio-20-earth-summit-brazil

Müller-Rommel, F, 1994, Green parties under comparative perspective, Working Paper 99, www.icps.cat/archivos/WorkingPapers/WP_l_99.pdf

Mulugetta, Y, Jackson T, Van der Horst D, 2010, Carbon reduction at community scale, *Energy Policy*, 38, 7541–5

National Geographic, 2013, Climate refugees, http://education.nationalgeographic.com/education/encyclopedia/climate-refugee/?ar_a=1

NEAA (Netherlands Environmental Assessment Agency), 2009, *Co-benefits of Climate Policy*, Bilthoven: NEAA

NEF (New Economics Foundation), 2006, *Growth isn't working*, London: New Economics Foundation, www.neweconomics.org/publications/entry/growth-isnt-possible

NEF (New Economics Foundation), 2008, A green new deal: Joined-up policies to solve the triple crunch of the credit crisis, climate change and high oil prices, London: New Economics Foundation

Nerlich, B, Lien, M (eds), 2004, *The politics of food,* Oxford: Berg

NIC (National Intelligence Council), 2012, *Global trends 2030: Alternative futures*, Washington DC: NIC

Nordhaus, W, 2008, A question of balance: Weighing the options of global warming policies, London: Yale University Press

NWDA (North West Development Agency), 2004, *Merseyside employment land study*

O'Connor, D, 1998, Applying economic instruments in developing countries: From theory to implementation, *Environment and Development Economics* 4, 91–110

O'Riordan, T, Turner, K, 1983, An annotated reader in enviornmental planning and management, Oxford: Pergamon Press

OECD (Organisation for Economic Cooperation and Development), 2002, Indicators to measure decoupling of environmental pressure from economic growth, Paris: OECD

Oreskes, N, 2004, Science and public policy: What's proof got to do with it?, *Environmental Science and Policy* 7, 369–83

Osbaldiston, R, Sheldon, KM, 2003, Promoting internalised motivation for environmentally responsible behavior: A retrospective study of environmental goals, *Journal of Environmental Psychology* 23, 349–57

Ostrom, E, 1990, The evolution of institutions for collective action, Cambridge: Cambridge University Press.

Ostrom, E, Burger, J, Field, CB, Norgaard, RB, Policansky, D, 1999, Revisiting the commons: Local lessons, global challenge, Science 9 April, 278–82

Owens, S, 2000, 'Engaging the public': Information and deliberation in environmental policy, *Environment and Planning A* 34, 1141–8

Parsons, W, 1995, *Public policy: An introduction to the theory and practice of policy analysis*, Cheltenham: Edward Elgar

Pattberg, P, 2005, What role for private rule making in global environmental governance? Analysing the forest stewardship council (FSC), *International Environmental Agreements: Politics, Law and Economics* 5, 2, 175–89

Pearce, DW, Turner, RK, 1990, Economics of natural resources and the environment, Hemel Hempstead: Harverster Wheatsheaf

Peattie, S, Peattie, K, 2009, Social marketing: A pathway to consumption reduction?, *Journal of Business Research* 62, 2, 260–8

Pelletier, N, 2010, Of laws and limits: An ecological economic perspective on redressing the failure of contemporary global environmental governance, *Global Environmental Change* 20, 2, 220–8

Pielke, RA, 2004, When scientists politicize science: Making sense of controversy over *The Skeptical Environmentalist*, *Environmental Science and Policy* 7, 5, 405–17

Pigou, AC, 1932, *The economics of welfare*, 4th edn, London: Macmillan

Ratner, BD, 2004 'Sustainability' as a dialogue of values: challenges to the sociology of development, *Sociological Inquiry*, 74, 1, 50–69

Redclift, M, 2005, Sustainable development (1987–2005): An oxymoron comes of age, *Sustainable Development* 13, 212–27

Redclift, M, Benton, T (eds), 1994, *Social theory and the global environment*, London: Routledge

Redclift, M, Woodgate, G, 1994, Sociology and the environment: A discordant discourse in M Redclift, T Benton (eds) *Social theory and the global environment*, London: Routledge

Redclift, M, Woodgate, G, 2010, *The international handbook of environmental sociology*, 2nd edn, Cheltenham: Edward Elgar

Roberts, J, 2011, *Environmental policy*, 2nd edn, London: Routledge

Roberts, JT, Parks, BC, 2007, *A climate of injustice: Global inequality, North–South politics, and climate policy*, Cambridge, MA: MIT

Rockström, J, Steffen, W, Noone, K et al, 2011, A safe operating space for humanity, *Nature* 461, 472–5

Rye, T, Ison, S, Santos, G, 2003, Implementing road pricing perfectly: Will London confirm the theory?, Paper presented at the AET Conference, http://abstracts.aetransport.org/paper/download/id/1575

Sanne, C, 2002, Willing consumers – or locked-in? Policies for sustainable consumption, *Ecological Economics*, 42, 273–87

SCEP (Study of Critical Environmental Problems), 1970, *Man's impact on the global environment: Assessment and recommendations for action*, Cambridge, MA: MIT Press

Schneider, SH, Rosencranz, A, Mastrandrea, MD, Kuntz-Duriseti, K, 2010, *Climate change, science and policy*, Washington, DC: Island Press

Schumacher, EF, 1973, *Small is beautiful: A study of economics as if people mattered*, London: Blond and Briggs

Schwela, D, Haq, G, Huizenga, C, Han, W, Fabian, H, Ajero, M, 2006, *Urban air pollution in Asian cities: Status, challenges and management*, London: Earthscan

Sharp, L, 1999, Local policy for the global environment: in search of a new perspective, *Environmental Politics* 8, 4, 137–59

Shaw, M, Davey Smith, G, Thomas, B, Dorling, D, 2008, The Grim Reaper's road map: An atlas of mortality in Britain, Bristol: Policy Press

Shove, E, 2010, Beyond the ABC: Climate change policy and theories of social change, *Environment and Planning* A 42, 6, 1273–85

Silva, RA, West, JJ, Zhang, Y et al, 2013, Global premature mortality due to anthropogenic outdoor air pollution and the contribution of past climate change, *Environmental Research Letters* 8, 034005, doi 10.1088/1748-9326/8/3/034005

Simon, HA, 1957, *Administrative behavior (2nd ed.)*, New York, NY: MacMillan.

Slaper, H, Velders, GJ, Daniel, JS, de Gruijl, FR, Van der Leun, JC, 1996, Estimates of ozone depletion and skin cancer incidence to examine the Vienna Convention achievements, *Nature* 384, 6606, 256-8

Smeets, E, Weterings, R, 1999, *Environmental indicators: Typology and overview, Technical Report 25*, Cophenagen: European Environment Agency, pp 1–20

Smith, A, 1776, *An inquiry into the nature and causes of the wealth of nations: A selected edition*, (edited by Sutherland, K, 1996) Oxford: Oxford University Press, p 50

Snell, C, 2008, Climate change and climate change policy 2006–7, in T Maltby, P Kennett, K Rummery (eds) *Social policy review 20*, Bristol: Policy Press

Snell, C, 2009, *The impact of Local Agenda 21 in England, and the implications for participation strategies*, Saarbrücken: VDM Publishing

Snell, C, Quinn, C, 2011, International development and global poverty, in T Fitzpatrick (ed) *Understanding the environment and social policy*, Bristol: Policy Press

Snell, C, Thomson, H, 2013, Reconciling fuel poverty and climate change policy under the coalition government, *Social policy review*, Bristol: Policy Press, 23–46

Snellen, ITM, Van de Donk, WBHJ (eds), 1998, *Public administration in an information age: A handbook*, Amsterdam: IOS Press

Spaargaren, G, 2003, Sustainable consumption: A theoretical and environmental policy perspective, *Society and Natural Resources* 16, 687–701

Spangenberg, JH, Lorek, S, 2002, Environmentally sustainable household consumption: From aggregate environmental pressures to priority fields of action, *Ecological Economics* 43, 127–40

Staats, HJ, Harland, P, 1995, *The EcoTeam program in the Netherlands. Study 4: Longitudinal study on the effects of the EcoTeam program on environmental behaviour and its psychological backgrounds*, Leiden, The Netherlands: Centre for Energy and Environmental Research, Leiden University

Stamminger, R, 2004, Is a machine more efficient than the hand?, *Home Energy* May/June, 18–22, www.landtechnik-alt.uni-bonn.de/ifl_research/ht_1/homeenergy_0504_dishwashing.pdf

Steffen, W, Grinevald, J, Crutzen, P, McNeil, J, 2011, The Anthropocene: Conceptual and historical perspectives, *Philosophical Transactions of the Royal Society A*, 369, 842–67

Steinberger, JK, Krausmann, F, Eisenmenger, N, 2010, Global patterns of materials use: A socioeconomic and geophysical analysis, *Ecological Economics* 69, 1148–58

Stern, N, 2006, The economics of climate change: The Stern review, Cambridge: Cambridge University Press, pp 27

Sutton, PW, 2007, *The environment: A sociological introduction*, Cambridge: Polity Press

Tang, B, Wong, S, Lau, M, 2008, Social impact assessment and public participation in China: A case study of land requisition in Guangzhou, *Environmental Impact Assessment Review* 28, 1, 57–72

Tews, K, Busch, P-O, Jörgens, H, 2003, The diffusion of new environmental policy instruments, *European Journal of Political Research* 42, 569–600

Thaler, RH, Susntein, CR, 2008, *Nudge: Improving decisions about health, wealth and happiness*, New Haven, CT: Yale University Press

Thøgersen, J, 1999, Spillover process in the development of a sustainable consumption pattern, *Journal of Economic Psychology* 20, 53–81

Thøgersen, J, Ölander, F, 2002, Human values and the emergence of a sustainable pattern: A panel study, *Journal of Economic Psychology* 23, 605–30

Thøgersen, J, Ölander, F, 2003, Spillover of environmentally-friendly consumer behaviour, *Journal of Environmental Psychology* 23, 225–36

Tisdell, C, 2001, Globalisation and sustainability: Environmental Kuznets curve and the WTO, *Ecological Economics* 39 185–96

Toke, D, 2011, UK Electricity Market Reform: Revolution or much ado about nothing?, *Energy Policy* 39, 12, 7609–11

Transport and Health Study Group, 2000, Carrying out a health impact assessment of a transport policy: guidance from the transport and health study group, www.fph.org.uk/policy_reports

Tscherning, K, Helming, K, Krippner, B, Sieber, S, Gomez y Paloma, S, 2011, Does research applying the DPSIR framework support decision-making?, Land Use *Policy* 29, 102–10

Turner, D, Hartzell, L, 2004, The lack of clarity in the precautionary principle, *Environmental Values* 13, 4, 449–60

Turning Point, 2003, *Social marketing and public health: Lessons from the field*, Turning Point, Seattle, WA: Turning Point

UN, 2006, *From water wars to bridges of cooperation: Exploring the peace-building potential of a shared resource*, www.un.org/events/tenstories/06/story.asp?storyID=2900

UN, 2012, World population day, www.un.org/en/events/populationday/

UN, 2013, Water for life decade, www.un.org/waterforlifedecade/quality.shtml

UNCED (United Nations Conference on Environment and Development), 1992a, Rio Declaration on environment and development, www.un.org/documents/ga/conf151/aconf15126-1annex1.htm

UNCED, 1992b, *Agenda 21: The United Nations programme of action from Rio*, New York: United Nations

UNDESA (United Nations Department for Economic and Social Affairs), 2011, *World population prospects: The 2010 revision. Highlights and advance tables*, New York: UNDESA

UNDP (United Nations Development Programme), 2008, Climate change and human development, video clip, http://www.youtube.com/watch?v=pwlUejanhzY

UNEP (United Nations Environment Programme), 2007, *Global environmental outlook 4*, New York: UNEP

UNEP, 2010, *Climate change*, accessed at www.unep.org/climatechange/Portals/5/documents/Factsheets/Climate_change.pdf

UNEP, 2011, *Towards a Green Economy: pathways to sustainable development and poverty eradication*, Nairobi: United Nations Environment Programme

UNEP, 2012, *Global environment outlook 5*, Nairobi: United Nations Environment Programme, www.unep.org/geo/geo5.asp

UNEP, 2013, *Disasters and conflicts*, www.unep.org/pdf/brochures/DisastersAndConflicts.pdf

UNEP, ND, *Environmental governance*, www.unep.org/pdf/brochures/EnvironmentalGovernance.pdf

UNEP/Water Supply & Sanitation Collaborative Council/WHO (World Health Organization), 1997, *Water pollution control: A guide to the use of water quality management principles*, www.who.int/water_sanitation_health/resourcesquality/watpolcontrol.pdf

UNEP/WCMC (World Conservation Monitoring Centre), 2013, *What is biodiversity?*, www.unep-wcmc.org/what-is-biodiversity_50.html

UNEP/WMO (World Meterological Organisation), 2011, *Integrated assessment of black carbon and tropospheric ozone summary for decision makers*, Nairobi: UNEP and WMO

UNESCO (United Nations Educational and Scientific Organisation), WWAP (World Water Assessment Programme), 2012, *Water development report 4*, Paris: UNESCO

UNFCCC (United Nations Framework Convention on Climate Change), 2009, Copenhagen accord: Decision -/CP.15 15. The conference of the parties, http://unfccc.int/files/meetings/cop_15/application/pdf/cop15_cph_auv.pdf

UNFCCC, 2011, Establishment of an ad hoc working group on the Durban Platform for Enhanced Action: Proposal by the President, http://unfccc.int/files/meetings/durban_nov_2011/decisions/application/pdf/cop17_durbanplatform.pdf

UNFCCC, 2012a, *Background on the UNFCCC: The international response to climate change*, http://unfccc.int/essential_background/items/6031. phphttp://unfccc.int/essential_background/items/6031.php

UNFCCC, 2012b, *First steps to a safer future: Introducing the United Nations Framework Convention on Climate Change*, http://unfccc.int/ essential_background/convention/items/6036.php

UNFCCC, 2012c, *Making those first steps count: An introduction to the Kyoto Protocol*, http://unfccc.int/essential_background/kyoto_protocol/ items/6034.php

UNFCCC (United Nations Framework Convention on Climate Change), 2012d, *Joint implementation projects*, http://ji.unfccc.int/JI_Projects/ ProjectInfo.htmlhttp://ji.unfccc.int/JI_Projects/ProjectInfo.html

UNFCCC, 2012e, *Joint implementation*, http://ji.unfccc.int/index.htmlhttp:// ji.unfccc.int/index.html

UNFCCC, 2012f, *The Mechanisms under the Kyoto Protocol: Emissions Trading, the Clean Development Mechanism and Joint Implementation*, http:// unfccc.int/kyoto_protocol/mechanisms/items/1673.php

UNFCCC, 2013, Feeling the heat: Climate science and the basis of the convention, http://unfccc.int/essential_background/the_science/ items/6064.php

UNGA (United Nations General Assembly), 2012, *The future we want*, www.un.org/ga/search/view_doc.asp?symbol=A/RES/66/288&Lang=E

UNPD (United Nations Population Division), 2010, *World population prospects: The 2010 revision*, UNPD, http://esa.un.org/wpp/ Documentation/WPP%202010%20publications.htm

Walker, G, 2012, *Environmental justice, concepts, evidence and politics*, London: Routledge

Walker, G, Fairburn, J, Smith, G, Mitchell, G, 2003, *Environmental quality and social deprivation phase II: National analysis of flood hazard, IPC industries and air quality*, Bristol, UK: Environment Agency

Wallace, AA, Flemming, PD, Wright, AJ, Nesbitt Irvine, K, 2010, Home energy efficiency grants and advice: Findings from the English Midlands, *Local Environment: The International Journal of Justice and Sustainability* 15, 5, 403–17

Ward, H, 2006, International linkages and environmental sustainability: The effectiveness of the regime network, *Journal of Peace Research* 2006, 43, 149

WCED (World Commission on Environment and Development), 1987, *Our common future*, Oxford: Oxford University Press

Wells, DT, 1995, *Environmental policy:A global perspective for the twenty-first century*, Upper Saddle River, NJ: Prentice-Hall

WFP (World Food Programme), 2013a, Hunger, www.wfp.org/hunger/causes

WFP, 2013b, *Hunger and climate change*, http://documents.wfp.org/stellent/groups/public/documents/communications/wfp227909.pdf

White, D, Raeside, R, Barker, D, 2000, *Road accidents and children living in disadvantaged area: A literature review*, Edinburgh: The Scottish Executive Central Research Unit, www.scotland.gov.uk/Publications/2000/04/0c1a7de7-fee6-47a3-af0b-56e90b39ea8f

White, PCL, Ford-Thompson, AES, Snell, CJ, Harris, S, 2011, Economic, environmental and social dimensions of alien vertebrate species in Britain, in D Pimentel (ed) *Biological invasions: Economic and environmental costs of alien plan, animal and microbe species*, 2nd edn, Boca Raton, FL: CRC Press

WHO (World Health Organization), 2003, *Climate change and human health: Risks and responses. Summary*, www.who.int/globalchange/publications/cchhsummary/en/index.html

WHO, 2005, Health effects of transport related air pollution, WHO: Demark (regional office)

WHO, 2010, 10 facts on preventing disease through healthy environments, www.who.int/features/factfiles/environmental_health/en/index.html

WHO, 2012a, *10 facts about cholera*, www.who.int/features/factfiles/cholera/facts/en/index4.html

WHO, 2012b, *Cholera impacts*, www.who.int/topics/cholera/impact/en/index.html

WHO, 2012c, *Water-related diseases: Cholera*, http://www.who.int/water_sanitation_health/diseases/cholera/en

WHO (World Health Organization), 2012d, 10 facts on climate change and health, www.who.int/features/factfiles/climate_change/en/index.html

WHO, 2013a, *Air pollution*, www.who.int/topics/air_pollution/en/

WHO, 2013b, *Land degradation and desertification*, www.who.int/globalchange/ecosystems/desert/en/index.html

Willows, RI, Connell, RK (eds), 2003, Climate adaptation: Risk, uncertainty and decision-making. Part 2: risk and uncertainty, *UKCIP Technical Report*, Oxford: UKCIP, pp 43–53, www.ukcip.org.uk/wordpress/wp-content/PDFs/UKCIP-Risk-framework.pdf

WorldMapper.org, 2006, *Cholera deaths*, http://sasi.group.shef.ac.uk/worldmapper/display.php?selected=232

WRI (World Resources Institute), 2002, 2002–2004: *Decisions for the earth: Balance, voice, and power*, Washington, DC: WRI

Wurzel, RKW, 2010, Environmental, climate and energy policies: Path-dependent incrementalism or quantum leap?, German Politics 19, 3–4

WWF (Worldwide Fund for Nature), 2012, *Living planet report 2012*, Godalming: Worldwide Fund for Nature

WWI (World Watch Institute), 2011, *2011: State of the world. Innovations that nourish the planet*, Washington, DC: World Watch Institute

WWI, 2013, The state of consumption today, www.worldwatch.org/node/810

Wynne, B, 1994, Scientific knowledge and the global environment, in M Redclift, T Benton (eds) *Social theory and the global environment*, London: Routledge

Wynne, B, 1996, Misunderstood misunderstandings: Social identities and public uptake of science, in A Irwin, B Wynne (eds) *Misunderstanding science?*, Cambridge: Cambridge University Press

Yim, S, Barrett, S, 2012, Public health impacts of combustion emissions in the United Kingdom, *Environmental Science and Technology* 46, 8, 4291–6

Zalasiewicz, J, Williams, M, Haywood, A, Ellis, M, 2011, The athropocene: A new epoch of geological time?, *Philosophical Transactions of the Royal Society A*, 369, 835–41

Zhao, Y, He, C, Gong, L, Yao, H, 2009, *Production capacity loss of farmland during urbanization in Beijing*, China, China Land Science, doi CNKI:SUN:ZTKX.0.2009-07-016

Index